P9-DMA-391

A B-47 Stratojet soars skyward with a JATO (jet-assist take-off) boost.

U.S. AIR FORCE

COVER: *The Saturn rocket was experimentally launched on October 27, 1962. A main purpose of this largest space vehicle under development in the United States is to land men and several tons of equipment on the moon before 1970.*

CHRYSLER CORPORATION

FRONT ENDSHEET: *Probably the best-known symbol of freedom in the whole world is the Statue of Liberty, looking impassively down on New York Harbor, with the North (Hudson) River at her back. The East River (right) flows between the tip of Long Island and Manhattan Island, of which the Wall Street area is shown here.*

PORT OF NEW YORK AUTHORITY

CONTENTS PAGE: *Astronaut Edward H. White took a walk in space during a two-man Gemini mission in 1965. He stayed outside the spaceship for twenty minutes.*

WIDE WORLD

BACK ENDSHEET: *The Capitol in Washington, D.C., is the national symbol of democracy, for it is here that the representatives of all 50 states meet in both houses of Congress and express the will of those who voted for them in free elections.*

HERBERT LANKS, BLACK STAR

BACK-COVER CREDITS (TOP ROW): BOB HENRIQUES, MAGNUM; GEORGE ZIMBEL; UNITED PRESS INTERNATIONAL. (SECOND ROW): UNITED PRESS INTERNATIONAL; MISSILE AND SPACE DIVISION, GENERAL ELECTRIC COMPANY. (BOTTOM ROW): WIDE WORLD; UNITED PRESS INTERNATIONAL

"A knowledge of the past prepares us for the crisis of the present and the challenge of the future."

JOHN F. KENNEDY
From his special foreword in Volume 1

THE AMERICAN HERITAGE NEW ILLUSTRATED HISTORY OF THE UNITED STATES

VOLUME 16
AMERICA TODAY

By ROBERT G. ATHEARN
Professor of History, University of Colorado

CREATED AND DESIGNED BY THE EDITORS OF
AMERICAN HERITAGE
The Magazine of History

PUBLISHED BY
DELL PUBLISHING CO., INC., NEW YORK

CONTENTS OF THE COMPLETE SERIES

Foreword by JOHN F. KENNEDY
Introduction by ALLAN NEVINS
Main text by ROBERT G. ATHEARN

A MASTER INDEX FOR ALL 16 VOLUMES APPEARS IN THIS VOLUME

CONTENTS OF VOLUME 16

UNITED PRESS INTERNATIONAL

CHAPTER 46

THE COLD WAR

Americans greeted the end of World War II with strong emotions. They were relieved to have wartime tensions at an end, joyful over the victory, and above all impatient to get back to normal living. President Harry S. Truman commented that, although the American people "mobilize with unparalleled swiftness and energy" once they know they must fight, after the war they "are as spontaneous and as headlong in their eagerness to return to civilian life."

Their chief preoccupations during the next months were with getting the troops home and out of uniform and with satisfying the wants—for household appliances, automobiles, and luxuries—pent up under wartime restrictions. These desires led the nation into sharp domestic controversies over how fast to abandon rationing and price controls, over whether labor was being unreasonable in its demands for higher wages, and over whether the combination of rising wages and prices was creating dangerous inflation.

Thus preoccupied, Americans heeded or even noticed few developments on the international scene. Yet it was there that storm clouds were casting a shadow that deepened as gradually but as inexorably as nightfall. Its cause was the postwar policies of the Soviet dictator Joseph Stalin, who had put aside communism's battle with capitalism during the war and accepted the capitalist nations as allies. With the war's end, he reverted to advancing the interests of Russia and communism through force and deceit wherever possible. He found he could do it in several places, because of Russia's territorial gains and because the Western powers' recent cooperation with Russia had relaxed their wariness of her. Stalin imposed Communist dictatorships on the nations of Eastern Europe that his troops occupied at the end of the war, and he sought through subversion and threats of force to spread communism to the rest of Europe, to Turkey, and to Iran.

The Wall—stark, grim symbol of the cold war—was built in 1961 to prevent East Germans from escaping to freedom in West Berlin. It is 29 miles long and eight to 12 feet high. Here it seals off the Brandenburg Gate from the British sector. The barbed wire was put up to keep West Berliners out of a no man's land.

Moreover, he balked at carrying out agreements with the Allies, notably in his effort to destroy the four-power administration of conquered Germany.

Americans received their first clear warning of the gathering storm from Winston Churchill, the wartime prime minister of Great Britain. Speaking at Fulton, Missouri, in 1946, he said, "A shadow has fallen upon the scenes so lately lighted by the Allied victory. . . . An iron curtain has descended across the [European] Continent."

Under the Soviet thrusts, the wartime spirit of cooperation gradually gave way to hostility and competition —a worldwide confrontation between the Communist bloc and the free nations that still exists. Because it implied a constant threat of war but did not turn into a wide-scale armed conflict, it came to be referred to as the cold war.

It stopped short of shooting at first because the United States had the mighty and dreaded atomic bomb and the Russians did not. But they developed the A-bomb by 1949, far sooner than American experts had expected. Russia also almost matched the United States in developing the still more powerful hydrogen bomb a few years later. This nuclear arsenal on each side created a military stalemate that has mainly kept the cold war cold.

Whether Stalin, who died in 1953, would have recognized that war in these circumstances meant mutual destruction can only be surmised, but his successors did. Nikita Khrushchev, who became the Russian premier in 1958, and Aleksei N. Kosygin, who replaced him in 1964, proclaimed a policy of "peaceful coexistence" with the West. Communism still aimed for domination, however. As Khrushchev once said, "The day the Communists abandon their drive to liberate the world will be the day the shrimp has learned to whistle on the mountaintop." Even so, Soviet Russia's boldest move—the 1962 attempt to set up a missile base in Fidel Castro's Cuba—was quickly retracted in the face of American power.

Struggle in Europe

Hardly two years after World War II, the Communists were in power in Albania, Bulgaria, Hungary, Poland, Rumania, and Yugoslavia. They were menacing the free government in Greece, and Turkey felt uneasy about their attentions and intentions. Communist Parties in France and Italy showed increasing strength.

At length the West recognized the need for counteraction. In March, 1947, President Truman proclaimed what later became known as the Truman Doctrine. Its essence was the containment of communism. "It must be the policy of the United States," he told Congress, "to support free peoples who are resisting attempted subjugation." The plan was to ward off communism by sending military and economic help to the nations in its path. As a beginning, the President asked for and obtained from

French farmers give up old ways for new as they learn to use American-built tractors sent as part of the 1947 Marshall Plan to help revitalize Europe's economy.

Congress a $400,000,000 program of aid to Greece and Turkey.

Coincidentally, the United States undertook the much broader and heavier task of helping to rebuild the devastated economies of Western Europe. This venture was proposed at Harvard University in June, 1947, by Secretary of State George C. Marshall. The aim, he said, would be to reduce the "hunger, poverty, desperation, and chaos" on which communism thrives. The Marshall Plan poured $12,000,000,000 into Europe in the next four years and became the forerunner of the present far-flung American foreign-aid program.

American resistance to Communist inroads was almost certain to provoke some new Soviet thrust. In the spring of 1948, Russia precipitated one of the major encounters of the cold war by attempting to shut the West out of Berlin with a blockade, defying the agreements for four-power control of the city. It was a difficult situation for the West, because Berlin was 110 miles inside the Communist zone of Germany. The Western answer was a massive airlift of supplies to the beleaguered city. For nearly 11 months, the West kept up the flow of planes, and by the time the Russians lifted their blockade in May, 1949, the airlift had supplied the city with nearly 2,500,000 tons of food and coal.

The United States also recognized that there must be a military as well as an economic response to the Communist challenge. In 1949, the Western powers created the North Atlantic Treaty Organization, in which they grouped forces under a joint command. NATO by 1963 had 15 mem-

WIDE WORLD

Children stand on what remains of a bombed building in Berlin in 1948 to watch an American plane delivering its cargo of coal in the Berlin airlift.

bers and a large military establishment, predominantly American. It had never reached its full potential as an association of equals and was even then losing unity and importance. Charles de Gaulle's France, having gained its own nuclear capability, withdrew its military support from the alliance in 1966 and forced other NATO troops to leave its soil in 1967. But NATO had served a vital function by providing an on-the-scene deterrent to Communist expansion in Europe.

Containment of communism was the best that could be hoped for, as America realized in 1956 when Hungarians revolted against Communist rule. Although the United States had encouraged the people behind the iron curtain to shake off Communist shackles, there seemed to be no effective way of aiding the Hungarian effort short of atomic war. As a result, Americans had to stand by and watch Soviet troops put down the courageous but hopeless revolt.

Berlin remained an issue fraught with recurring tension. Beginning in 1958, Khrushchev showed again and again that he could precipitate a crisis there at any time. In November of that year, he demanded that the West get out of Berlin, leaving it a "demilitarized, free city." He set six months as the time limit.

President Dwight D. Eisenhower's response to the Soviet ultimatum was to make it unmistakably clear that he was ready to go to war over Berlin. Khrushchev temporized, but continued to restate his demands in various ways and set new deadlines. When he found American determination as strong under President John F. Kennedy as under President Eisenhower, he avoided pressing the issue to a showdown.

Struggle in Asia

Communism made one of its most formidable gains in 1949, in Asia. After a long and bitter civil war in China, the Communists under Mao Tse-tung overthrew the Western-backed Nationalist government of Chiang Kai-shek, who fled to the island of Formosa with the remnants of his army. Thus there fell to communism a truly gigantic prize—a country with an area exceeded only by Russia's and a population greater than that of any other.

In control of the heartland of Asia, and under militant leadership, the Communists began the same kind of effort as in Europe—to gain territory, or at least influence, through force and subversion. In less than a year, they brought on one of the great show-

UNITED PRESS INTERNATIONAL

The tomb of an unknown refugee, shot by Communists as he swam toward freedom, was placed as a memorial by West Berliners where it can be seen from East Berlin.

UNITED PRESS INTERNATIONAL

In snow and freezing weather, a machine gun—its emplacement set into a Korean hill facing the Communist forces—is about to be fired by American soldiers.

downs of the cold war—a hot war in Korea.

That country had been divided after World War II into Communist and democratic sectors. On June 25, 1950, troops of Communist North Korea struck into South Korea behind a spearhead of Soviet tanks. President Truman responded immediately with an American force and also obtained quickly—because the Russians were boycotting the Security Council and therefore could not exercise their veto—a United Nations resolution making the effort to halt the Communist attack a U.N. action. After initial setbacks, the U.N. force under General Douglas MacArthur swept the Communists back almost to the border of China. Then the Chinese poured massive forces of "volunteers" into the conflict, and that produced a stalemate almost where the war had started—along the 38th parallel. An armistice, worked out in 1953 after President-elect Eisenhower had kept a campaign promise to go to Korea, ended the conflict.

But that did not deter Communist thrusts into other parts of Asia. A particularly hot spot was Indochina, then under French rule. The Communists, bidding for control of an independence movement, began in 1946 a bitter civil war against the French in the part of Indochina that is now Vietnam (the other parts being Laos and Cambodia). Despite extensive Ameri-

UNITED PRESS INTERNATIONAL

While fulfilling a campaign promise to make an inspection tour of Korea, Eisenhower eats his chow with men from the front.

can aid, the French by 1954 were defeated. An international conference at Geneva subsequently divided Vietnam, leaving the North under Communist control and the South under an anti-Communist regime buttressed to a constantly increasing degree by the United States. This backing was deemed necessary because of a Southern revolutionary movement that North Vietnam supported, supplied, and finally augmented with troops.

SEATO—the Pacific NATO

A direct result of the Communist thrusts in Southeast Asia was an expansion of the Western alliance system. At the urging of the United States, eight nations formed the South East Asia Treaty Organization in 1954. The members—the United States, Great Britain, France, Australia, New Zealand, Pakistan, the Philippines, and Thailand—agreed to act jointly against Communist aggression and to build up the military and economic strength of the region.

Although SEATO, having only three Asian members and operating over a vast area, failed to achieve the effectiveness and strength of NATO, the Communists made no major gains in Asia after its creation. Threatening invasion, Communist China bombarded the offshore islands of Quemoy and Matsu with artillery fire, but American shows of force and promises to help the Nationalist Chinese defend the islands stabilized the situation. China's attacks along its lengthy border with India in 1962 pushed neutral India temporarily toward the West and ended in a truce. A strong thrust by the Communist Pathet Lao in Laos was halted in 1962 as Russia, Britain, and America agreed to neutralize the country. In 1963, Cambodia declared it would no longer accept American aid and, in 1965, broke diplomatic ties with the United States; Prince Sihanouk said that Cambodia would not turn Communist unless attacked, but it soon became a refuge for Vietcong soldiers. Indonesia, under President Sukarno, bitterly opposed the newly organized nation of Malaysia and threatened to ally with China in an anti-Western movement. Sukarno pulled Indonesia

WIDE WORLD

United States Marines search for Vietcong in a marsh in South Vietnam. More than 460,000 American servicemen were stationed in Vietnam by the autumn of 1967.

out of the United Nations in 1965, but after Indonesian Communists—backed by Sukarno and China—attempted to take over the government, the Indonesian army seized control, purged the Communists, and slowly eliminated Sukarno's powers.

But for America the main conflict in Asia was in South Vietnam. The republic, proclaimed in 1955 by Ngo Dinh Diem, suffered from unstable rule and guerrilla warfare by the rebel Vietcong. President Diem, who had failed to make necessary reforms, was assassinated in 1963. By June, 1965, eight different governments had ruled. That month the head of the South Vietnamese Air Force, Nguyen Cao Ky, became premier; his regime survived longer than all eight predecessors combined.

The major reason for his survival was the vastly increased military commitment of the United States. Not long before President Kennedy died (there were 25,000 American military advisers in Vietnam at the time, and it was thought by many that the rebellion would soon be put down) he indicated that he doubted the value of backing a government that governed badly. Nevertheless, the United States took the position that the Vietcong represented a threat of Communist Chinese expansion. Furthermore, it was undeniable that the government of North Vietnam was giving aid and encouragement to the Southern rebels.

The major questions were whether or not the Vietcong and North Vietnam were actually extensions of Peking communism; would American withdrawal from South Vietnam encourage subversion in other areas of Southeast Asia; did the fate of Vietnam mean a great deal to United States interests; and should America be involved there at all? These questions continued to be debated with increasing ferocity at home and abroad after the administration of Lyndon Johnson decided to answer them in the affirmative. By mid-1967, there were 462,000 American troops in South Vietnam, and an estimated 50,000 North Vietnamese regulars. North Vietnam was being bombed almost daily from the air. The undeclared war was costing the United States billions of dollars each year. As part of an effort to strengthen the allegiance of the South Vietnamese to their government, a democratic-style constitution was drawn up by a nationally elected assembly, and elections for a president and legislature were held. In this, too, the United States had played a major role.

Encounter in America

Until 1962, all the great showdowns of the cold war occurred far from the United States. Then the Russians brought their weapons into the Western hemisphere with their bold gamble in Cuba, thereby causing the greatest threat to world peace since Korea. After Fidel Castro's successful six-year revolution, Cuba aligned itself with the Communist bloc, and received a steady supply of aid from Russia. This led to an attempted invasion of the island by anti-Castro refugees early in John Kennedy's Presidency. The United States had encouraged the landings at the Bay of Pigs and had trained the refugee force, but the invasion failed. Then, in the summer of 1962, American intelli-

BOB HENRIQUES, MAGNUM

Fidel Castro's speeches spellbound the Cubans after he came to power. But he soon became spellbound by Russian communism.

UNITED PRESS INTERNATIONAL

When Russia removed her missiles from Cuba in 1962, an American ship (foreground) steamed close alongside to inspect carefully the cargo on deck.

gence noted a sharp rise in Soviet shipments to Cuba. At first these seemed to include primarily defensive matériel, such as ground-to-air missiles. Evidently the three thousand Soviet "technicians" who had been sent to Cuba were training Cubans to use the new equipment. Soon, however, American photo-reconnaissance began uncovering something much more ominous—hastily built bases armed with missiles that could carry nuclear warheads to most cities of the Western Hemisphere. There also were clusters of Soviet IL-28 jet bombers.

Kennedy's response to the threat was a "quarantine," which in effect was a naval blockade supported by constant air surveillance. The purpose was to halt and turn aside any Soviet ships found to be carrying offensive weapons to Cuba. The President declared also that the United States would insist on "prompt dismantling and withdrawal" of the offensive installations already in Cuba.

With the two great powers in that toe-to-toe stance, the world braced for a major collision, if not in the Caribbean then at some place like Berlin if the Russians chose to bring counterpressure in an area where they had the geographical and military advantage that the United States had on its side of the Atlantic. It seemed highly unlikely that Russia, having boldly penetrated the Western Hemisphere, would agree to withdraw.

Yet withdraw the Russians did. On October 28, Premier Khrushchev said they would dismantle the missile bases and remove the missiles and bombers. Within days, the bases had disappeared and Russian ships apparently carrying the missiles and bombers were outbound from Cuba. Khrushchev later said that his aim had been to prevent an American invasion of Cuba, and that he considered the 1962 episode a victory for communism. Whatever his true motives, he had not been willing to start a nuclear holocaust. President Kennedy's decision to enact a quarantine rather than to order an immediate shooting response had given Khrushchev time to back out gracefully.

Global competition

Besides the direct confrontations in Europe, Asia, and the Americas, the West and the East were competing in many other parts of the world—and even in outer space. Each side sought to win over the other, and the bystander nations, to its way of life.

For both sides, an important part of this effort was to win the support, or at least to preserve the neutrality, of the nations whose policy was one of nonalignment in the cold war. Here Russia had an advantage, for many of the unaligned nations had only recently gained their independence, after years as colonies of European powers. Usually in these countries there was bad feeling toward the former masters, and that feeling was often directed toward America as well, because of her close associations with Europe. So in many parts of the world—Southern Asia, the Middle East, North Africa—there were countries or factions willing to be impressed by Russia's wooing with trade and aid and her propaganda about Western "imperialism."

Russia may have been disappointed in the results of these tactics, for they produced no major gains for communism except in Cuba. But they did cause difficulties for the United States by fostering anti-Western sentiment and by stirring up strong pro-Communist movements in many nations.

It could be argued that some of Russia's failures came from overplaying her hand. Communism's strong-arm methods, as used in Hungary and China and Berlin, warned the new nations that if they embraced Russia too wholeheartedly, they would find themselves in the grip of a far harsher colonialism than Europe's. Moreover, most of the new nations so desperately needed trade and foreign aid to build up their shaky economies that they had to look to the United States as well as to the Soviet Union for it.

But undoubtedly the chief reason for the poor Russian showing was the massive and widespread American aid program. Between the end of World War II and 1966, the United States provided economic and military assistance in excess of $102,000,000,000 to more than one hundred nations.

One of the most remarkable aid programs was the Alliance for Progress, a ten-year plan offered to the nations of Latin America by President Kennedy in 1961. Pointing out that Communist subversion thrives on poverty, Kennedy emphasized that the widespread poverty in Latin America was the result of a social structure that centered wealth and political power in the hands of a few. American aid, he said, would therefore be contingent upon democratic reforms and self-assistance by the recipient governments. Under President Lyndon Johnson this condition was somewhat modified, and economic aid was provided before social reform was instituted. The administration of the program was consolidated, internal-improvement projects were added, and the President promised that

A twenty-two-year-old Peace Corps volunteer from the state of Minnesota teaches English at a high school for girls in Kabul, which is the capital of Afghanistan.

WIDE WORLD

United States support of the Alliance would continue indefinitely.

The American foreign-aid program included not only money, military assistance, and supplies, but also civilian specialists who helped the developing nations acquire modern techniques of manufacturing and farming. The Peace Corps, also created during the Kennedy administration, sent American volunteers to nations that asked for them. Peace Corps men and women served as teachers, science advisers, nurses, and in similar capacities. Many were assigned to live in impoverished villages and help the peasants with basic problems of farming and health. It was a new and productive way of winning friends in foreign countries.

Another element of the East-West competition was the space race. After the orbiting of Sputnik I in 1957, the United States and Russia strove to surpass each other in space achievements. From modest beginnings, they progressed to putting manned spacecraft in orbit, practicing rendezvous and docking in space, and experimenting with man's ability to maneuver outside an orbiting spaceship. Instrumental and photographic exploration of the moon and other planets was begun. The goal of America's Project Apollo was to land men on the moon by 1970. But it was evident by 1967 that both sides were having second thoughts about the cost and were wondering just how far the competition should go: after the moon, where would they race to? There was talk of combining American and Russian efforts, but such cooperation seemed unlikely.

COMBAT ART SECTION, U.S. NAVY

The Polaris missile, perhaps the best deterrent in the Western arsenal, is fired from a submarine in a painting of a test.

Search for peace

The existence of nuclear weapons made a major war between the United States and Russia, if not unthinkable, definitely something to be avoided. At the United Nations, through normal diplomatic channels, and in "summit" meetings of top leaders, negotiations went on. The efforts produced some memorable incidents. In 1959, Premier Khrushchev visited the United States, toured the country for 12 days, and then conferred with President Eisenhower at the vacation White House, Camp David, in Maryland. Less than eight months later an American photo-reconnaissance aircraft, flown by Major Francis Gary Powers, was shot down over Russia. At a summit meeting that followed almost immediately, Khrushchev furiously denounced President Eisenhower and broke up the conference. In September, 1960, Khrushchev attended a meeting of the United Nations General Assembly and, in one unforgettable moment, took off a shoe and banged it on the desk in displeasure at a speech by the Philippine delegate.

But the intransigence with which the Russians faced their capitalist antagonists did not completely obscure a growing willingness to do business with the West. A hopeful sign of *détente* was given in 1963. The two major powers were worried that through alliance or research many more countries might gain nuclear capability, thus vastly increasing the danger of a nuclear war. There was also great concern over radioactive fallout from nuclear tests. So the Soviet Union, Great Britain, and the United States worked out a treaty that banned all such tests in the atmosphere and under water. Ninety-nine other nations signed the treaty; the only major holdouts were Charles de Gaulle's France and Communist China. The treaty did not solve all the problems, but it was a beginning.

Another useful move was the Kennedy administration's decision to discard dependence on massive retaliation in favor of a more balanced military force. With a wider range of choices before it, the United States would not necessarily have to employ nuclear weapons in any major war of the future. To lessen the chance of a war begun by accident—through a misunderstanding or the failure of highly complex equipment—a hot line (teletype and radio system) was set up between Washington and Moscow in August, 1963. (During the dangerous crisis in the Middle East in the spring of 1967, the two powers kept in close touch over the teletype.)

Late in 1963, on the heels of a Soviet crop failure, the United States agreed, for the first time in the cold war, to sell wheat to Russia. These indications of relaxing tensions between the Iron Curtain countries and the West could be traced, in part, to the common cultural and historical heritages of the European Communist nations and the Western powers; Russia and her satellites also wished to devote more energy and money to their domestic needs. But it was due as well to a split in Communist ranks. China had grown impatient with peaceful coexistence, and was not ready to rule out nuclear war as a way to achieve its will. The Chinese began to challenge Russian leadership of the movement, and emerged as a threat to world peace and prosperity. A Russian-American *détente* was therefore particularly desirable.

UNITED PRESS INTERNATIONAL

During a state visit of the Kennedys to France, they and the de Gaulles appear together (center, foreground) at the theater in the Palace of Versailles on June 1, 1961.

In the effort to establish a lasting peace the United Nations continued to play an important role. That organization had built-in limitations, however. It could not offend any of the major powers without endangering its very existence. The Charter embodied this fact of life by giving to World War II's major allies—the United States, the Soviet Union, Great Britain, France, and Nationalist China—permanent seats on the Security Council and the right to veto the Council's decisions. In 1950, however, an American-sponsored resolution partially removed that stumbling block by providing that if the Security Council were prevented by veto from acting "where there appears to be a threat to the peace," the General Assembly could be called into session on 24 hours' notice at the request of any seven members of the Security Council—now nine, since the enlargement, in 1966, of the Council from 11 to 15 members.

There was also no practical way to get member nations to pay their share for United Nations peace-keeping efforts. The provision in the Charter that was aimed at ensuring this financial support said that if any country fell more than two years behind in its payments, it would lose its vote in the Assembly. But if the delinquent nation happened to be a major one, depriving it of its right to vote would severely cripple the whole organization. Russia, France, and a number of other countries refused to pay their

President Lyndon Johnson and Soviet Premier Aleksei Kosygin confer in Glassboro, New Jersey, in June, 1967. Their meeting was helpful, but produced no concrete results.

share of the costs of peace-keeping in the Congo and in the Gaza Strip, and as a consequence the Assembly meetings of 1964 and 1965 became deadlocked; no issue could be brought to a vote because a showdown on payments and voting rights would be faced. The United States, which regularly paid one-third of the United Nations budget and had tried to sustain the Charter provision, finally backed down in August, 1965, and agreed to ignore it for the sake of the life of the United Nations.

The world organization lacked a meaningful police force to see that member nations obeyed its resolutions, and had no way to compel unified political or economic action against any country whose behavior it disapproved. The United States had consistently opposed the admission of Communist China to the world organization. Thus the United Nations had little power in the Far East, since Communist China did not recognize the U.N.'s diplomatic authority. In the Middle East, both Russia and the United States helped to arm the Arabs and Israelis, and thus contributed to the explosion of violence there in 1967. The U.N. had not been able to eliminate border fighting in the Middle East in the ten years since the Suez Crisis, having only a small armed force at its command. When the United Arab Republic demanded the removal of the peace-keeping force from the border between itself and Israel, the United Nations was legally required to comply, and did. When war broke out again, the U.N. had no way of forcing on the combatants the immediate cease-fire for which it quickly voted.

Even so, the U.N. served a useful function as a forum for airing disputes. Though various countries tried to use it to promote national aims, it was at least a dependable diplomatic center, with a number of peace-keeping successes to its credit. Furthermore, its continued existence provided hope for an eventually stronger world organization.

The long pull

Ultimately, world leaders knew, peace and a viable United Nations depended, first on a *détente* between the two leading powers, and then on the self-sufficiency of other nations. When a country is weak, or when a large part of its population suffers from hunger, poverty, or political oppression, it issues, in effect, an invitation to outside forces or internal revolutionaries to take advantage of it—to try to change it, to disrupt its peace. Should the United States and the Soviet Union reach a productive working agreement, stabilization of the emerging nations and the improvement of living conditions around the globe would undoubtedly be one of their major goals.

There were hopeful signs on both sides by the summer of 1967. Disarmament talks had been underway at Geneva for many years. A ban on all nuclear tests—including subterranean explosions—and restriction of the spread of nuclear weapons were also under discussion. The key nations were the Soviet Union and the United States, for together they could impose a settlement on the rest of the world.

Among other signs of accommodation were an agreement permitting direct commercial flights between New York and Moscow; the concerted effort by Russia and the United States to convince the Burmese diplomat, U Thant, to stay on as secretary-general of the United Nations; the moves being made to widen trade between the West and the Iron Curtain countries, and the treaty that permitted the United States and Russia to open more consulates in the other's cities. In the United Nations a treaty guaranteeing the peaceful use of outer space was worked out.

Cooperation in these areas continued despite major disagreements between the two nations. The war in Vietnam was the chief source of trouble. Russia would never have looked with favor on the American attempt to keep South Vietnam non-Communist. But the Chinese challenge to Russian primacy in the Communist camp made it extremely difficult for Russia not to take as hard a position on the war as China's. Thus it refused to act as a mediator, supplied North Vietnam with equipment (including ground-to-air missiles), and used the issue as another excuse to cry "*Nyet!*" at the conference table. But this did not represent a basic freeze in relations. When the Arabs and Israelis began threatening war in the Middle East, the United States and the Soviet Union took opposite sides and sent naval forces into the Mediterranean. Russia openly backed the Arab states she had been arming. The United States played a waiting game, declared its neutrality, and watched with relief—if not with surprise—as the Israeli army streaked to a stunning victory in six days. Despite their outward displays of strength and the Soviet Union's subsequent campaign to force the Israelis to give back all the territory they had won in the fighting, it was worth noting that the two major powers had avoided any part in the shooting, communicated often, and were exceedingly careful not to upset each other during the crisis. A summit conference held by Johnson and Premier Kosygin (who had come to New York to urge the United Nations to condemn Israel as the aggressor) at Glassboro, New Jersey, produced no concrete results but indicated that both sides were willing to discuss their differences. As Johnson said, "it does help a lot to sit down and look a man right in the eye and try to reason with him. . . ."

Still, it was safe to conjecture that a real alliance between them, if it was ever to develop, was a considerable distance in the future. So the United States worked in several other directions to protect its interests and improve the chances of peace. One of the movements that took on increasing importance as a stabilizer was the removal of trade barriers between nations, such as tariffs. In Europe were the Common Market of the "inner six" and the European Free Trade Association of the "other seven". The American contribution was the "Kennedy Round" at Geneva, Switzerland, which, after long negotiations, produced in 1967 tariff cuts amounting to an average of 33 per cent by nearly 50 non-Communist nations.

In Asia the United States was indicating readiness to consider a change in its policy toward China, and to accept a future Asia not dominated by the West if China did not dominate it either. In Latin America, United States aid was augmented by an increased respectfulness toward the needs of individual countries, as evidenced by the writing of a new canal treaty that treated Panama as an equal. Thus, as the cold war began to thaw into what many hoped would be a new season in world politics, American foreign policy appeared to be growing more and more flexible.

SPECIAL PICTURE PORTFOLIO

MARSHALL SPACE FLIGHT CENTER

THE WORLD OF OUTER SPACE

Just as man was once impelled to explore the great seas of the earth and search for lands beyond the horizon, so he is reaching out today into the immense oceans of space and the "lands"—the planets and stars—they contain. The rewards are great—new knowledge, military advantage, economic gains, national prestige. Billions of dollars and the work of many scientists are going into varied efforts to conquer the greatest frontier man has ever challenged. Already, with the complex instruments he fires aloft, he has learned much. Indeed, he is already using space for such practical matters as weather observation and communications. But he must learn more, which means he must go out into space itself. Undaunted by vast distances and uncertain hazards, he is now building the vehicles and systems that will take him to the moon. An example of the scale on which he is working is shown above—the first stage of a Saturn rocket that will power the first American moon flight.

THE RUSSIANS PROCLAIM THEIR PROWESS IN SPACE

ALL: SOVFOTO

This cover from the Russian magazine *Krokodil* typifies the jubilation with which the people of the U.S.S.R. have celebrated their many successes—including numerous firsts—in the exploration of space. Here the tribute is to Yuri Gagarin for his pioneering orbit of the earth on April 12, 1961. In August of the same year, Gherman Titov made 17 orbits; in 1962, two other Russians made 48 and 64 orbits in double flight. The four cosmonauts were given highest honors and sent on tours of both the Soviet Union and foreign countries to call attention to Russia's achievements in the early days of the space age.

The Russians put the first man-made object into orbit around the earth when they launched Sputnik I in October, 1957. It circled the earth at a distance of 140 to 560 miles for three months. A model of it is shown at the left. At the right is the much more elaborate Sputnik III (which orbited 17 months) in a Soviet exhibition in East Germany.

Cosmonaut Gagarin, in his space suit, is shown just before take-off. His flight took him in an orbit 108 to 187 miles out, and he reached a top speed of some 17,000 miles an hour—the fastest man had traveled.

Valentina V. Tereshkova, 26—a former textile worker whose parachuting hobby led her into the Russian space program —was the first woman to orbit the earth, 48 times in 70 hours and 50 minutes.

At Cape Kennedy (formerly Cape Canaveral), Florida, launching a man into space calls for long, meticulous preparation, and the final days and hours are devoted to a minute checking-out of all that has been done. During the last moments, a "cherry picker" crane (above) has its cabin right next to the capsule, ready to take the astronaut out and away in case anything goes wrong. When all is ready, there comes the spectacular blast-off (below).

AMERICA SENDS ITS ASTRONAUTS ALOFT

An astronaut's gear is cumbersome. His suit is individually tailored for him, but it contains or is attached to many kinds of equipment to protect him against heat and cold, or loss of pressure or oxygen. These pictures show Colonel John H. Glenn (above) in his capsule during a triple orbit; below, left, Commander Walter M. Schirra, Jr., entering his capsule for a six-orbit flight; below, right, Major Gordon Cooper aboard the *Kearsarge* after a 22-orbit mission.

ALL: NATIONAL AERONAUTICS AND SPACE ADMINISTRATION

A NEW "VOICE" FOR MAN

A striking example of how man has already put his space research to practical use is Telstar. This is an orbiting "package" of instruments that receives radio impulses from one point on earth and relays them to another. Because of its position far outside the earth's atmosphere, which often interferes with electronic communication, Telstar's signals are clear and reliable. The drawing (right) shows the principle: A TV program originating at the far right is shot up to Telstar, which amplifies it and sends it on to a special receiver; there, it is fed to a regular TV broadcasting station. Below is a giant antenna (the flylike man on the framework gives the scale) that picks up Telstar's signals. At the lower right is a conception of how a chain of Telstars would serve all parts of the world simultaneously.

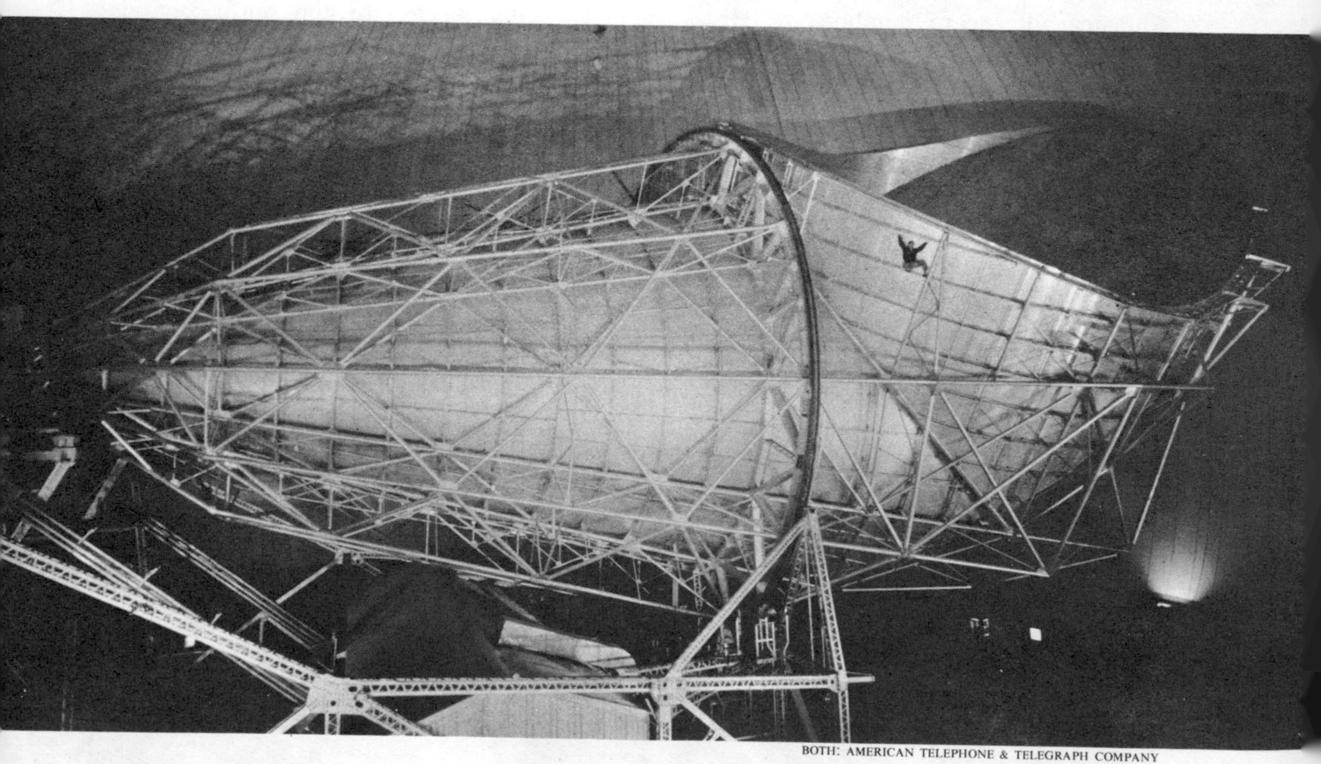

BOTH: AMERICAN TELEPHONE & TELEGRAPH COMPANY

WALTER HORTENS—*The New York Times*

NEW VENTURES, NEW TECHNIQUES

NATIONAL AERONAUTICS AND SPACE ADMINISTRATION

At times, it seems as if man's imagination were running away from his ability to make things really happen. But achievement follows achievement, and actual "hardware" takes the place of a scrawl on a blackboard. The shapes that emerge can be beautiful or grotesque. The huge but graceful device above is an antenna, receiving information from the weather satellite Tiros.

The time of traffic jams in space is far off (if, indeed, it ever comes), but the rate of launchings for different purposes increases apace. The drawing at the right suggests how busy the realms of space may one day become. A probing capsule (upper left) has been sent out from its parent space station (inset) to sample the trail of a comet; in the distance are other capsules.

MISSILE & SPACE DIVISION GENERAL ELECTRIC COMPANY

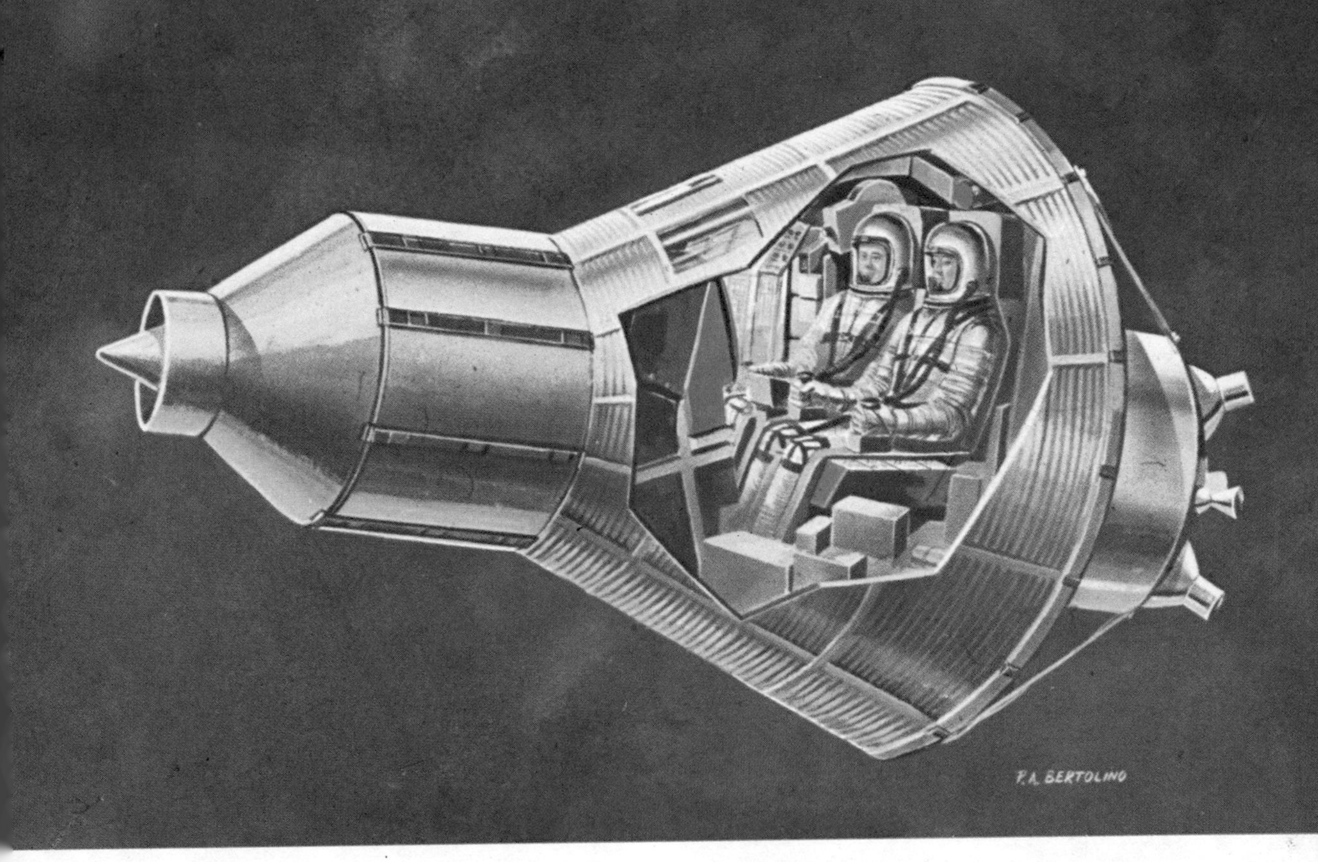

As the United States was finishing its one-man orbital program, it was already engaged in its two-man Gemini, or twins, flights. The purposes of the Gemini project included the conducting of experiments aimed at bringing about a rendezvous in space of two vehicles, a "walk in space" by an astronaut, and scientific observation more detailed than one man could make.

FACTS, NOT FANCIES

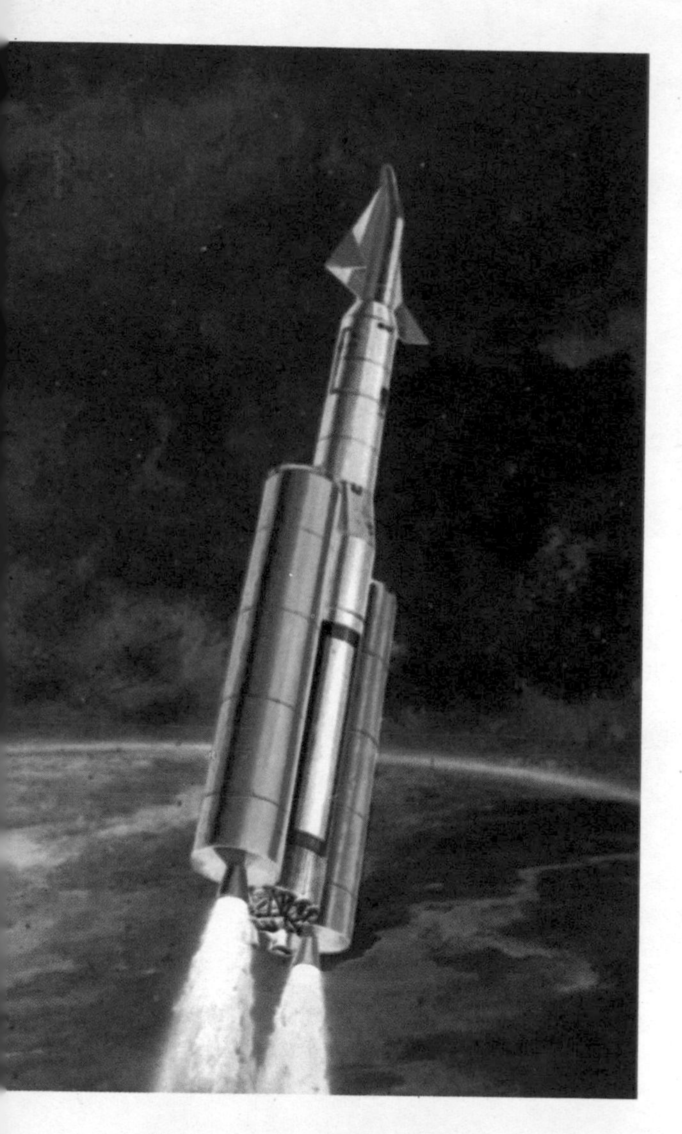

To avoid the necessity of a separate launch from earth for each mission, the scientists are devising "way stations" in space. Maintaining a steady orbit of the earth, they would serve as refueling and maintenance stops and training stations for space crews, observatories, and laboratories. The version shown above rotates about its big hub to provide an artificial gravity. At the center a small spacecraft leaves its "dock."

The range of scientists' interests in exploring space is immensely wide, and the tools they need are many. One thing they want to do is to move inside and outside the vague boundary between the earth's atmosphere and the beginnings of space, to allow prolonged study. For a while, scientists were hopeful that the manned space-air vehicle called DynaSoar(above) would provide maneuverability; that idea was abandoned, however.

Although photographs taken by Mariner IV in 1966 indicated that there was probably no life on Mars, scientists still hoped to discover some living things (if only simple plants) there. The drawing at right shows what a manned research station might be like. Inside, the atmosphere would simulate earth's; outside, men would wear heavy boots with their space suits, to compensate for the low gravity on Mars.

ALL: MISSILE & SPACE DIVISION, GENERAL ELECTRIC COMPANY

UNITED STATES

MIGHTIEST BOOSTER

To launch longer and more complex space flights—including a manned moon shot—the United States began work in 1957 on a super-rocket named Saturn. Using clusters of engines rather than a single giant one, scientists at Huntsville, Alabama, brought the Saturn through a series of successful performances. The early, two-stage model was called Saturn I. Later, the Saturn V was developed: it had three stages and its 7,500,000-pound lift-off thrust was five times that of Saturn I. Its first launching was set for late 1967. The painting of a Saturn on its launch pad (left) shows a spare second stage in the foreground. On the right a Saturn is fired statically; below, a test flight is prepared.

ALL: MARSHALL SPACE FLIGHT CENTER

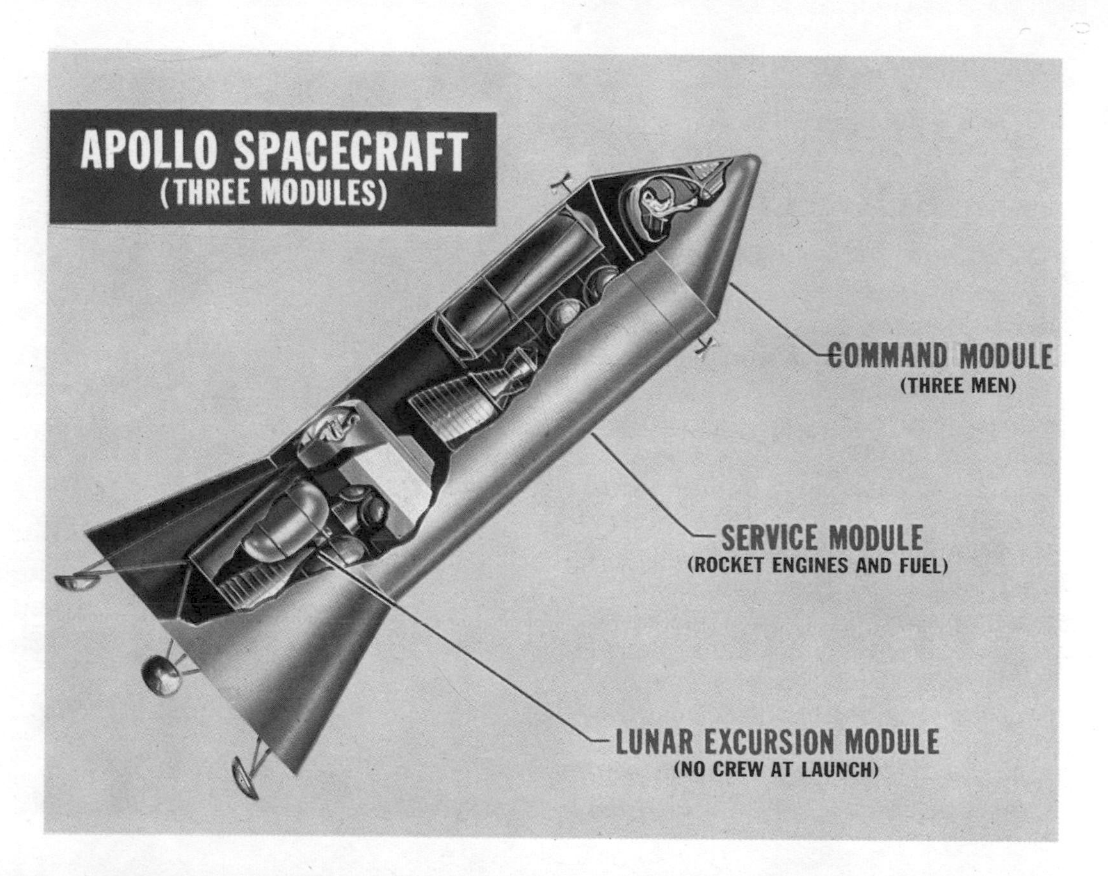

ALL: MARSHALL SPACE FLIGHT CENTER

TO THE MOON . . .

Man's greatest adventure—greater than the feats of any previous explorers because it will take him out of his own, natural, terrestrial environment—will be his leap to the moon. The American plan for it—Project Apollo—calls for a three-man crew to be shot out in a complex vehicle (left) that will separate into its several components at various times. Then, hopefully, these pieces will maneuver, rendezvous, rejoin, and separate again, and only the smallest—the conical command module—will return to earth.

The Apollo vehicle is shown in the drawing at the lower left, perched atop the mighty three-stage Saturn just after the firing button has been pushed. The whole assembly weighs some 3,000 tons, including fuel, at this point. The first and second stages and part of the third will carry the spacecraft into a "parking orbit" of the earth (upper right), where it can be checked out, then the rest of the third stage will kick the vehicle out in an "escape velocity" (escaping the pull of the earth's gravity). Each rocket stage falls away as it burns out. As the Apollo vehicle speeds toward the moon, the lunar excursion module (LEM) separates but follows the same trajectory. The command and service modules maneuver and make a nose-to-nose rendezvous. Either through an air lock or by stepping out into space in their protective suits two men transfer to the LEM, and it heads down (right, center) toward the moon, while the other two modules remain in a close orbit. Before touching down, the LEM hovers (lower right) with its own engines to pick a safe landing spot. The photographic missions of the Surveyor satellite have proven that the pock-marked lunar surface will be suitable for landing.

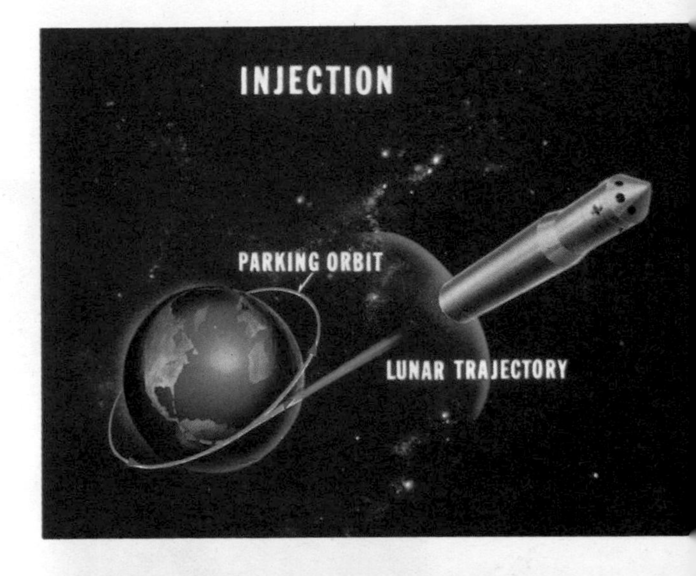

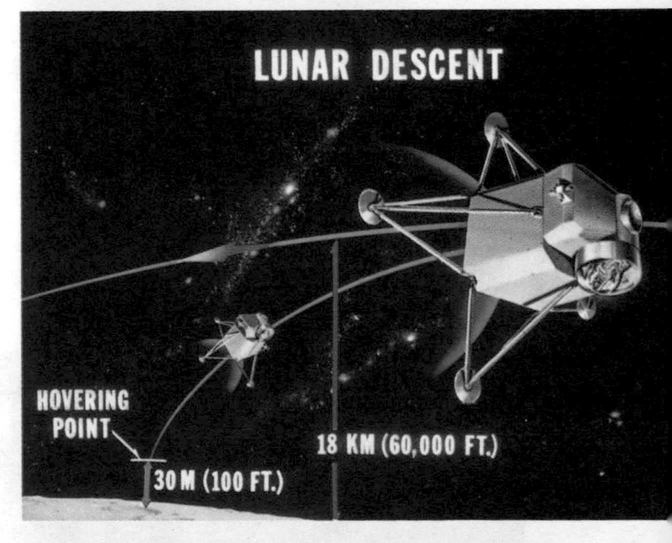

...AND SAFELY BACK TO EARTH

For the return flight, the stilt-legged base of the LEM serves as a launch pad, is left on the moon. Small rockets overcome the moon's low gravity. The LEM capsule (upper part) joins up with the command module. The two "moon men" enter it, jettisoning the capsule. Nearing earth (below), the command module drops the service module and turns for re-entry.

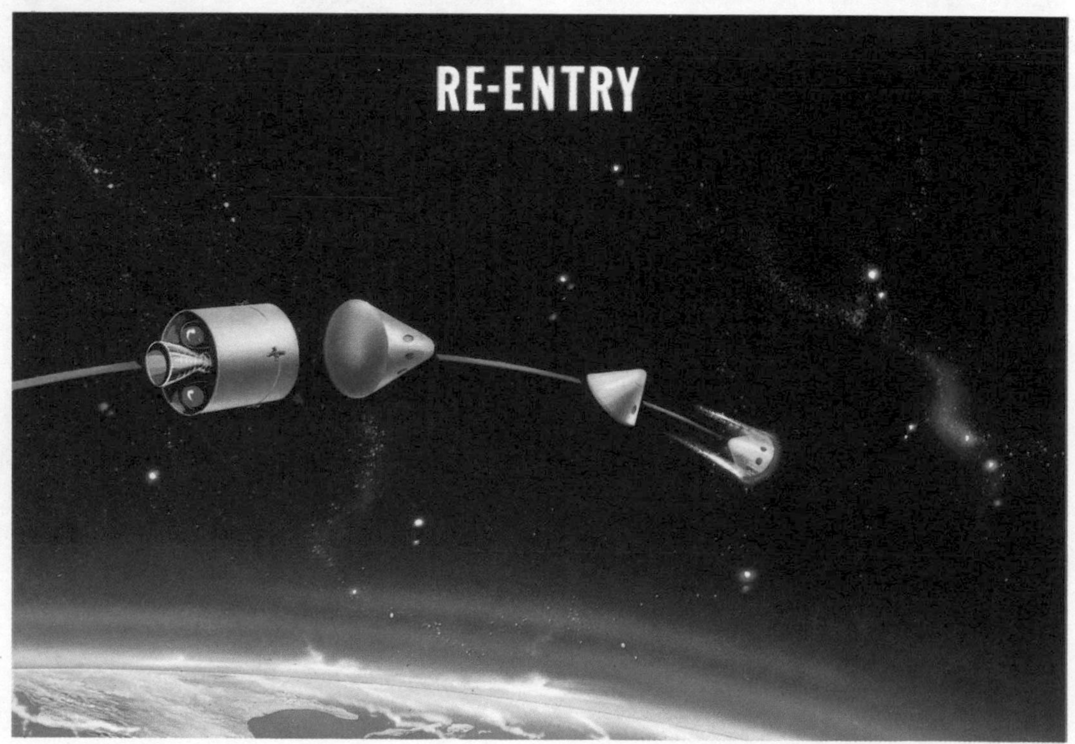

ALL: MARSHALL SPACE FLIGHT CENTER

Unless a maneuverable craft is developed, the command module will re-enter the earth's atmosphere at a precisely determined time and angle, so that it will land in a chosen area. At several thousand feet over that area, a canister in the pointed nose drops off, releasing huge parachutes (above). Land impact (rather than sea) is planned, for easier recovery.

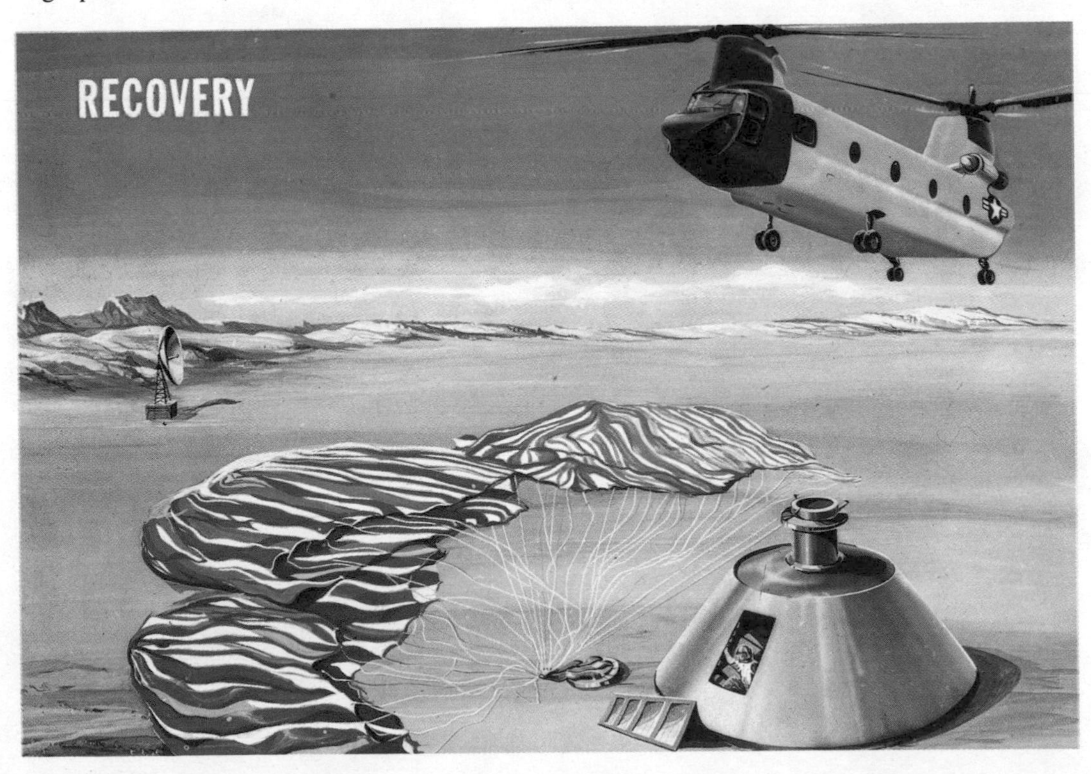

PEARSON MARINA
Owens

CHAPTER 47

THE DOMESTIC SCENE

Although the cold war dominated the postwar years, it was the kind of problem that remained somewhat remote from the day-by-day activities and thoughts of most Americans. It was diffuse and far away. There was little any citizen could do about it unless he was one of the federal officials directly concerned. What interested him primarily, therefore, were questions closer to his daily life—making a living, maintaining his and his family's health, educating his children, enjoying his leisure, improving his community. Occasionally he might think about the cold war and worry about it, especially when it altered or threatened to alter the course of his existence, as in the Korean War and the Cuban crisis. But mostly it was in the background, and when he thought beyond his own concerns, it was usually about America's domestic affairs.

The popularity of the boat show in New York's Coliseum in 1963 epitomizes the surplus wealth of America that is available for "conspicuous consumption"—free to be spent on luxuries for leisure enjoyment.

Of these there were many. The nation grew enormously after 1945—by more than 59,000,000 in population, to an estimated 196,000,000 early in 1967, and more than triple in gross national product, from $213,500,000,000 to $681,207,000,000. It saw science and technology advance by seven-league strides, bringing such everyday wonders as the transistor radio and the jet plane, and, even more significantly, transforming industry, agriculture, medicine, and many other aspects of life.

Growth and change entailed, as usual, conflict over their direction and pace. There was debate on whether the traits that had always distinguished Americans—energy, self-reliance, inventiveness, resourcefulness—had changed, too. But prosperity, strength, and vigor pervaded the American scene. In his 1963 State of the Union message, President Kennedy told the 88th Congress, "I can report to you that the state of this old but youthful nation is good."

Political developments

Elections often turn more on tradition and personalities than on issues. That of 1946 was one in which issues played an important part. There was widespread dissatisfaction with the Truman administration's handling of domestic problems. Demobilization was one of them. Even though the armed forces dropped from the 12,300,000 of the wartime peak to 1,500,000 at the beginning of 1947, servicemen and their families complained of delays and inequities in demobilizing. Price controls were another lively issue; President Truman was virtually alone in wanting to maintain them. His insistence was blamed for a shortage of meat, which occurred at a time when exasperated Americans felt they had had enough of shortages and restrictions and regulations.

The Republicans exploited these feelings skillfully ("Had enough?" they asked) and won a sweeping victory in the Congressional elections. The line-up in the incoming 79th Congress had been Democratic 56 to 39 in the Senate and 242 to 192 in the House; the 80th Congress was Republican by 51 to 45 in the Senate and 245 to 189 in the House. It was one of the major reversals in an American election and seemed to assure a Republican Presidential victory in 1948, for the first time in 20 years.

Republican confidence grew as a result of Truman's performance in 1947-48. By pressing civil-rights legislation, he so alienated Southerners that a substantial group of them formed a States Rights' Democratic Party, which quickly acquired the name Dixiecrats, and nominated a Presidential ticket headed by Governor J. Strom Thurmond of South Carolina. Conversely, the left-wing faction of the Democratic Party, concluding that Truman's program was not liberal enough, formed a Progressive Party and nominated for President Henry A. Wallace, who had been Vice-President before Truman and briefly a Truman cabinet member. With two major factions of the Democratic Party thus disaffected, it seemed certain that the Republicans would breeze into the White House.

In the circumstances, the "regular" Democrats were somewhat reluctant to nominate Truman. They did so, however, as much because repudiating their own President would be an acknowledgement of bankruptcy as for any other reason. The Republicans nominated the man who had made a strong run against President Roosevelt in 1944—Governor Thomas E. Dewey of New York. There then began one of the most remarkable Presidential contests of modern times.

Dewey conducted his 1948 campaign as if his election were assured. He showed little inclination to deal specifically with the issues. He was serene and aloof in manner. Truman, on the other hand, carried his campaign to the people with a series of whistle-stopping tours in which he laid into the Republicans so vigor-

It was Truman's hard campaigning, much of it at whistle stops like this one in Idaho (above), that gave him his victory in 1948. The day after election, he gleefully displays the Chicago Tribune*'s premature headline (below).*

BOTH: UNITED PRESS INTERNATIONAL

BOTH: UNITED PRESS INTERNATIONAL

On his way to becoming President, John F. Kennedy (on the rostrum) thanks his supporters for nominating him at the 1960 Democratic convention in Los Angeles.

ously that it became commonplace for people in the crowds to cry, "Give 'em hell, Harry!" as he spoke.

Even so, the political analysts expected Dewey to win. They were confounded by the outcome. Truman carried 28 states with 303 electoral votes, Dewey 16 states with 189, the Dixiecrats four Southern states with 39.

Elected President in his own right, and with a Democratic Congress, Truman pressed a program that he called the Fair Deal and described as "an extension of the New Deal." It emphasized civil-rights and social-welfare legislation. But the conservative coalition in Congress found the program distasteful and adopted little of it.

That opposition was probably an accurate reflection of the country's mood, for it was a time of prosperity and domestic normalcy, and there was far less enthusiasm than in New Deal days for social reform. Also, the Democrats had won five straight Presidential elections, and the feeling grew that it was time for a change. On top of that, there were during the last years of the Truman administration numerous revelations of corruptness and laxness on the part of high government officials. Republican cries of a "mess in Washington" had the sound of an effective campaign issue.

It proved to be effective in 1952, as did the slogan "Time for a change," but even more effective was the candidate nominated by the Republicans —General Dwight D. Eisenhower, the immensely popular wartime com-

The television debates between Kennedy and Nixon in 1960 helped put the lesser-known Senator before the nation and established a new form of campaigning.

mander in Europe and postwar NATO commander. Eisenhower won easily over Governor Adlai E. Stevenson of Illinois, an urbane and witty candidate (so much so as to alienate some voters) but one running on the record of an administration that had lost favor. The Eisenhower victory was of such proportions (442 to 89 electoral votes) that he carried a Republican Congress into power with him.

Eisenhower came to the Presidency declaring that his aim for the federal government was "trying to make it smaller rather than bigger and finding things it can stop doing instead of seeking new things for it to do." He did attempt to cut expenditures and to persuade the states to take over some of the responsibilities that had lodged in Washington. But he made little headway. It is probable that no President could, for in a huge and growing country, heavily engaged with defense and foreign commitments, a big federal government would appear to be an inescapable fact of life.

Eisenhower also brought to office a concept of the Presidency that differed sharply from that of his two Democratic predecessors. He thought the President should try to remain above partisan strife, be a conciliator of conflicting interests, and concern himself more with carrying out the enactments of Congress than with proposing new programs. To his critics, this was an abdication of leadership; to supporters, it was just what the country needed after 20 years of hard-driv-

SPERRY RAND CORPORATION—ERICH HARTMANN

The Univac III Data Processing System, being checked before delivery, will do the work formerly done by several people.

ing, strongly partisan chief executives.

The public seemed mostly indifferent to this controversy. They liked Eisenhower the man. The essentially personal nature of his popularity was especially evident in 1956, when he handily defeated Stevenson again (457 to 74 electoral votes) while the G.O.P. failed to win either branch of Congress. It was the first time since 1848 that the man elected President had been unable to carry into office with him a majority in at least one of them. But Eisenhower had Democratic Congresses in six of his eight years as President, and the relatively smooth relationship between the White House and the Capitol during those years suggested that the President and the dominant group in Congress—led by House Speaker Sam Rayburn and Senate Majority Leader Lyndon B. Johnson—were more of the same mind and more in tune with the country than the difference in their political labels might indicate.

Probably Eisenhower could have been elected easily to a third term if he had been eligible and willing to run. But he was ineligible, as the first President affected by the two-term Constitutional amendment proposed in 1947 by the Republican 80th Congress (mindful of Franklin Roosevelt's four terms) and ratified in 1951. So the Republicans turned almost automatically in 1960 to the youthful Richard M. Nixon, who had been Eisenhower's Vice-President. The even more youthful Senator John F. Kennedy campaigned without stint for the Democratic nomination and won it against a large field of opponents.

Kennedy faced some obstacles. He was a Catholic, running in the face of a tradition that no Catholic had been or could be elected President in a predominantly Protestant country. And he was less known than Nixon. But Kennedy overcame these obstacles by the vigor and astuteness of his campaign—particularly in an unprecedented series of face-to-face television debates with Nixon. These made him as well-known as Nixon and showed him to be at least equally articulate and well-informed. He won by 303 to 219 electoral votes but was only 118,574 popular votes ahead of Nixon

RICHARD SAUNDERS, SCOPE ASSOCIATES

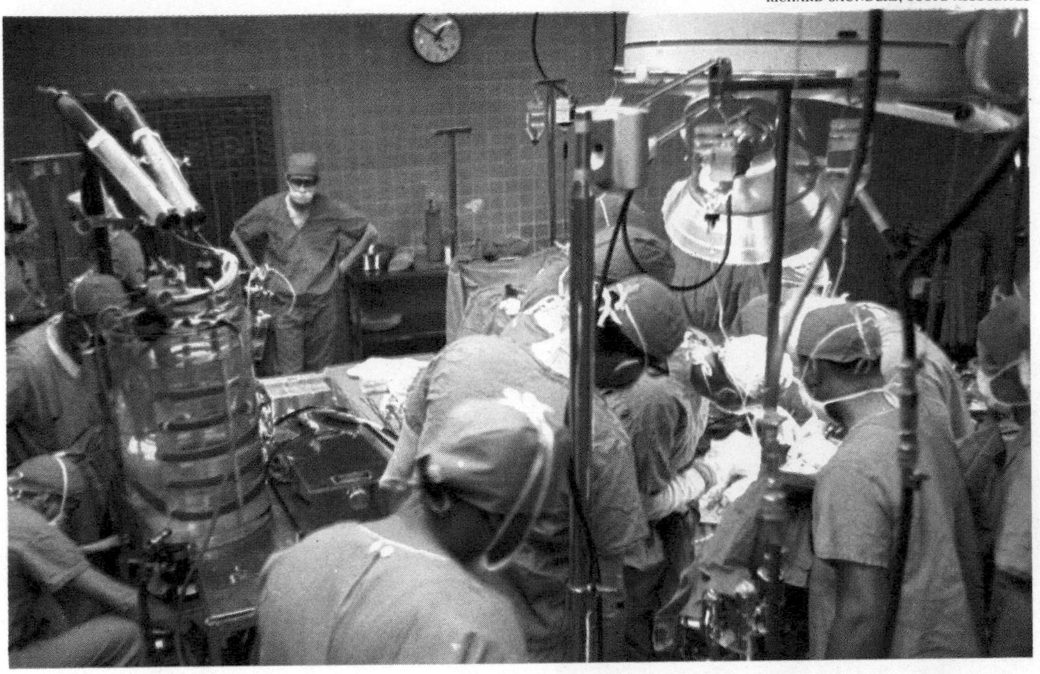

Open-heart surgery is performed at a New York hospital. Because of the heart-lung pump oxygenator (left), longer, more complex operations are now possible.

out of the record 68,500,000 cast.

As President, Kennedy espoused the concept of a leader "in the thick of the battle." He showered Congress with proposals, both foreign and domestic. Several were highly controversial. He sought to expand the Social Security system to include a "medicare" program of help to the aged in the payment of certain health-care expenses. He wanted to inaugurate the first across-the-board program of federal aid to public elementary and secondary schools—but he excluded private schools at those levels (most of which are Catholic parochial schools) and thereby precipitated a sharp debate over whether the aid should include private schools. In 1963, he presented a revolutionary budget involving a deliberate deficit of $11,900,000,000, which would be caused largely by a tax cut. He argued that the tax cut would be the most sensible cure for a persistent sluggishness in the economy, for it would increase purchasing power and thereby increase business investment in plants and equipment. The stimulation thus given the economy would, he said, ultimately result in more tax revenues and a balanced budget.

But Kennedy was pressing these programs upon the same conservative coalition in Congress that Truman and Eisenhower had faced. Even though his party gained seats in both houses of Congress at the midterm

WIDE WORLD

Vice-President Hubert Humphrey and President Lyndon Johnson in the White House.

elections—the only time that had happened in the 20th century except for 1934, at the peak of the enthusiasm over the New Deal—he found persistent difficulty in winning Congressional approval for his programs.

Nevertheless, Kennedy's political strength was on an upswing in 1963. His successful handling of foreign crises and his efforts on behalf of Negroes, senior citizens, and the underprivileged had increased his prestige in most parts of the nation. Looking forward to the election of 1964—which he was confident of winning—he was anxious to solidify his leadership of the Democratic Party. It was during a trip to Texas—designed to unite warring factions in the party—that he was shot and killed in Dallas on November 22, 1963.

The crime stunned the world. But America rallied to bury its murdered President with ceremonies of dignity and honor, and efficiently transferred power to the new President, Lyndon B. Johnson. As Johnson told Congress, "This is our challenge—not to hesitate, not to pause, not to turn about and linger over this evil moment but to continue on our course so that we may fulfill the destiny history has set for us."

One of the most experienced politicians ever to reach the Presidency, Johnson was an altogether different sort of man from Kennedy. He was an expert in the arts of manipulation and bargaining. Combining his own skills with the willingness of most congressmen to build a legislative memorial to Kennedy, Johnson energetically engineered a spectacular series of legislative successes. The Civil Rights Act of 1964 and a tax cut—to name the most significant of many achievements—moved quickly from committee to law in Johnson's first year in office.

Despite his many years of public service, Johnson entered the Presidency as an unknown quantity. While his record in Congress had been generally conservative, he had, as Vice-President, worked tirelessly to advance the liberal causes of the Kennedy administration. As President, however, he announced that he would seek a national consensus, that he intended to be President of all the people. By the time the election of 1964 approached, he had gained the support of Negroes and intellectuals, farmers and labor, without losing the esteem of business. He lost support only in the South, which turned against President Johnson because of his championing of civil rights.

The Republican Party gave its 1964 presidential nomination to Senator Barry Goldwater. A conservative, he was convinced that Americans wanted "a choice, not an echo." Republicans, he said, had been nominating liberals for so long that many conservatives—perhaps enough to swing an election—did not even bother to vote. Johnson was anxious for a sweeping victory and election in his own right. He got it, losing only five Southern states and Goldwater's Arizona, and receiving the greatest popular plurality in electoral history. Moreover, the national repudiation of the Republican nominees cost the minority party one seat in the Senate and thirty-seven in the House.

After the election Johnson's "consensus" began to give way. The costs of the Vietnamese war soared, and many of his domestic "Great Society" expenditures were cut. The Republicans gained four Senate seats and forty-seven House seats in the 1966 elections and looked forward to an even greater recovery in 1968.

Internal security

With the advent of the cold war, and the clear evidence of how far Russia would go in attempts at subversion, the attitude toward whatever Communists and fellow travelers there might be in the American government changed drastically. A massive effort was begun to expose and get rid of them as foreign agents. Therein lay the roots of the bitter debate over internal security during the postwar decade, for although few persons quarreled with the objectives of the campaign, many protested the manner in which it was sometimes conducted.

The heart of the argument was over the effect of the anti-Communist movement on the civil liberties guaranteed to individuals under the Constitution. One group maintained that it was folly to be sensitive about the civil liberties of people who would destroy civil liberties if they ever came to power. The position of the other group was that if the Communist hunters were allowed to infringe civil liberties, they would undermine the very democracy they claimed to be protecting. The situation was complicated by two factors: First, in the anti-Communist movement there were political opportunists who were seizing on a popular issue mainly to advance their own careers. Second, some arch-conservative groups resorted freely to the technique of imputing Communist sympathies to anyone who disagreed with them.

There was indeed evidence in the years just after World War II that Communists had infiltrated the government, but to what extent no one was ever able to determine. The most celebrated case was that of Alger Hiss, once high in the Department of State. In 1948, Whittaker Chambers, a former Communist, testified before the House Un-American Activities Committee that before the war he had received stolen government documents from Hiss for transfer to Soviet authorities. Hiss denied the accusation under oath and was indicted for perjury. In his first trial, the jury was unable to reach a verdict, but he was convicted in 1950 and imprisoned. In 1949, Judith Coplon, a Department of Justice employee, was arrested and later convicted of espionage in behalf of the Soviet Union. (The conviction was reversed on appeal.)

Into that highly charged atmosphere there marched in 1950 the man who became the most controversial figure in the struggle over internal security—Republican Senator Joseph R. McCarthy of Wisconsin. He was virtually unknown until he made a speech at Wheeling, West Virginia, in February, 1950. There he declared that he had in his hand a list of 57 (or 205; the number was never clearly established, even by McCarthy) Communists in the Department of State. It was a spark in tinder, and thereafter McCarthy became the focal anti-Communist figure. He never did substantiate his famous "list." His habit when asked for proof was to move on to fresh accusations.

Many Americans, perhaps most, thought McCarthy was a demagogue. They regarded him as brazen, disdainful of the truth, and a master of innuendo. In their view, he was harmful to the government mostly because of the fear he instilled in such agencies as the Department of State with his roughshod investigations and blanket charges—all techniques that quickly became known as McCarthyism.

For four years McCarthy bestrode the stage. But in the end he was his own undoing. He bayed as loudly about Communists in government when the Republicans came to power as he had under the Democrats. In fact, he made more of a stir, because in the Republican 83rd Congress he conducted some flamboyant investigations as chairman of the Senate Committee on Government Operations and its Permanent Investigating Subcommittee. He discredited himself by attacking such prominent Americans as General George C. Marshall and President Eisenhower. In the spring of 1954, his committee investigated alleged subversion in the Army Signal Corps, and in nationally televised hearings he revealed to a wide audience his penchant for vituperation and invective. In August, the Senate appointed a special committee to look into charges concerning his behavior as a Senator, and in December, the Senate voted to "condemn" him for unbecoming conduct.

WIDE WORLD

The end of the investigations by Joseph McCarthy (left) came in 1954 when many of his fellow Senators, like Ralph Flanders (right), began to criticize him.

With that, McCarthy's influence was at an end. At almost the same time, the Supreme Court began issuing a series of decisions emphasizing the need to protect civil liberties in anti-Communist activities and curbing some of the more extreme practices of Congressional investigating committees. The furor over the internal-security issue subsided.

Labor problems

Organized labor's struggle for recognition was far in the past by the end of World War II. Congress, in the National Labor Relations Act of 1935—popularly known as the Wagner Act—had put the weight of law behind labor's right to organize in unions and to bargain collectively with employers. Thus by 1946 labor was in a strong position to press its point of view during the great rush to reconvert to a civilian economy, and it was well prepared to take returning servicemen into its ranks. Labor's attitude was that with prices rising, the wages of workers should rise, too. The result was an epidemic of strikes, which shut down for varying periods much or all of the nation's automobile, coal, railroad, airline, steel, shipping, and meat-packing industries.

The many strikes caused a widespread belief that labor had been given too much power by the Wagner Act. In 1947, the Republican 80th Congress passed, over President Truman's veto, the Taft-Hartley Act. Among other provisions, it outlawed the closed shop (in which the worker must be a member of the union in order to be hired); restricted the union shop (in which the worker must join the union within a certain time after being hired); and enabled the government to obtain court injunctions halting for 80-day "cooling-off" periods any strikes that threatened the national health or safety.

Labor reacted to the Taft-Hartley Act with a storm of denunciation. Union leaders called it a "slave-labor act" and demanded its repeal. But the mood of Congress was clearly otherwise, and the law stayed on the books, although with occasional modifications. Several states, indeed, went beyond Taft-Hartley and passed controversial "right-to-work" laws, which in effect outlawed the union shop by making it illegal to bar a man from working because he refused to join.

Actually, labor's biggest threat in the postwar years came not from laws but from automation—the trend in industry toward replacing, or displacing, manpower with complex

An automated aluminum rolling mill is electronically operated by only one man (center), who activates the machinery by means of a punched I.B.M. card.

machines, including those able to coordinate the work of other machines. One of the simpler examples was the operation of typesetting machines in newspaper plants by paper tapes, perforated in a central office and reproduced in widely separated places through electric transmission.

The trend to automation created one of the major social problems of the postwar period by dislodging hundreds of thousands of workers. At first they were mostly those who were unskilled or semiskilled, but as automation became more sophisticated—evolving electronic computers, or "brains," that could do such jobs as bookkeeping and filing—it began to make sharp inroads on the ranks of low-level white-collar workers as well. Although the work force continued to grow through the development of new products and the expansion of service businesses, the human problem of the workers who had been displaced and could not find new work was grave. Retraining programs attempted to help the older workers; for younger people, the emphasis was on increased education as a means of acquiring greater skills.

Automation had a marked impact on organized labor, for it tended to increase the proportion of salaried white-collar workers such as engineers and highly skilled technicians and decrease the proportion of paid-by-the-hour blue-collar workers, who traditionally have formed the bulk of union membership. Thus, even though labor managed to quiet a long period of internal conflict through a merger of the American Federation of Labor and the Congress of Industrial Organizations in 1955, union expansion slowed during the 1950s until eventually total membership hovered with almost no change at about 17,000,000—approximately one worker in four.

Many of the labor disputes of the '50s and '60s involved struggles over automation. Employers sought to reduce featherbedding, or jobs made unnecessary by the improvement of machines but continued at union insistence, and also looked for ways to introduce more efficient machinery in order to be less dependent on human labor. Unions tried to soften the impact of automation by protecting jobs or by working out plans with employers whereby men displaced by machines would be given other work.

As a result of automation and other conditions displeasing to labor, there was a series of major strikes in the early 1960s. One by longshoremen in 1963 immobilized the nation's shipping for 38 days after the expiration of a Taft-Hartley injunction and was settled only after the government had applied extraordinary pressure. At the same time, a printers' strike stopped publication for 114 days of the six largest newspapers of New York City—including the powerful New York *Times,* with its national and international circulation and influence, and the New York *News,* with more circulation than any other newspaper

UNITED PRESS INTERNATIONAL

May Day is celebrated in America and Russia: Above is a National League baseball game at San Francisco's Candlestick Park. Below is the May Day parade in Moscow's Red Square to commemorate the anniversary of the 1917 Revolution.

FRANK DONATO, PHOTO RESEARCHERS

in America. Several months after the end of that strike, the New York *Mirror* went out of business. Shortly after a 1965 strike—this one by the Newspaper Guild—three dailies, the *Journal-American*, the *World-Telegram & Sun*, and the New York *Herald-Tribune* merged into one. But the new paper failed in 1967.

New York City remained the center of labor unrest. A transit strike on January 1, 1966 paralyzed the city for twelve days, and a buildings-service union strike left many residents without elevator service and hot water for more than a week in 1967. Nevertheless, New York was in the vanguard of a national movement to end discrimination in labor unions, particularly in the construction and service trades.

The strikes of the '60s, in the opinion of many observers, negated efforts on the part of President Johnson to achieve repeal of certain restrictive passages of the Taft-Hartley Act—especially those sections forbidding the closed shop.

Farm paradox

There had been nothing like it in history—a huge and growing country consistently producing enormous surpluses of food despite strenuous efforts to curb the output of its farms. Soaring productivity was at once the pride and the bane of American agriculture. Despite sharp drops in the acreage planted (from 353,000,000 in 1950 to 310,000,000 a decade later) and in the number of farm workers (from 7,497,000 to 5,696,000 in the same period), total output and yields per acre continued to mount.

To a considerable extent, the reasons for this overabundant cornucopia were improvements in farm machinery and in fertilizers. But government price-support programs figured prominently in the situation, too. They had been started in the depression of the 1930s as a means of putting a floor under the income of farmers. As it was politically difficult to end the programs, they continued, and in time came to be a means of assuring farmers of a market. Surpluses had a price-depressing effect; with a support program, the farmers could always be sure of selling to the government if they could not find buyers in the open market. So by the 1960s, the government was spending $2,500,000,000 a year to support prices and was storing $5,500,000,000 worth of surplus commodities it had acquired under the program—a reservoir that included such inventories as a billion bushels of corn and more than a billion bushels of wheat.

Throughout the period there were sharp controversies over what to do about the problem. The Truman administration adhered to a policy of rigid and high supports, combined with production controls that usually required a farmer to hold his planting within a certain acreage limit in order to qualify for benefits. The Eisenhower administration favored a gradual re-

Endless and efficient farms like these in Nebraska, producing larger and larger crop surpluses, are a problem to the government in trying to keep prices stable.

turn to a free market, with supports reduced (to discourage overproduction) and controls relaxed. To that end, the administration proposed a system of flexible supports, but Congress limited the extent of the change in that direction.

President Kennedy tried at first to put through a system of high supports with strict controls on output. Under his plan, producers of the major surplus crops—wheat and feed grains—would have to accept rigid limits on both acreage and sales or lose supports. The curbs would be set to keep output below demand, and the government would make up the differences by selling from its surplus. In that way, the problems of both excess production and massive stored surpluses would be attacked. But Congress was reluctant to make any fundamental changes in farm programs.

Part of the grain surplus was sent to other countries in the mid-1960s. In 1964, wheat was sold to the Soviet Union; and in 1966–67 the effects of a massive famine in India were partially countered with donations of grain from America.

Business and science

The period of affluence into which the United States entered after World

HOWARD LEGG, SHOSTAL

War II produced an unprecedentedly high standard of living. The wartime economy was converted into a booming peacetime one, kept at fever pitch because of shortages that the war had brought about. To provide the housing, factories, commercial facilities, community services, and hospitals that the country needed, twenty years of intensive building activity began, and manufacturers were hard put to supply the demand for consumer goods. Ensuring continuation of the economic boom was the fact that Europe remained wartorn for several years and, being unable to provide for its own needs, was dependent on the United States.

In the late '50s a brief business recession temporarily halted the growth of prosperity; but in the '60s, stirred by an accelerated space program, the advent of commercial jet transportation, and an increase in international trade, the economy resumed its upward swing.

The success of "consumer capitalism" has not been the only triumph of modern America. Medicine has made giant strides in the prolongation of life and the improvement of health. The scourge of polio was virtually banished from the land after the introduction of the Salk vaccine in 1955 and the Sabin oral vaccine in 1962. Platoons of "wonder drugs" were developed to attack such once-dreaded diseases as tuberculosis and pneumonia. Surgeons learned how to transplant, preserve, and replace vital organs and perform lifesaving operations that had been beyond their knowledge before. Massive forces were marshaled with extensive federal help through the rapidly growing National Institutes of Health, to solve the riddles of cancer and circulatory diseases. Said the American Medical Association in 1962, "Medicine today is moving swiftly along with the Scientific Sixties—the decade, many scientists predict, when man is expected to learn to diagnose some illnesses with computers, predetermine his children's sex, and even transplant a human heart."

The achievements of medical research were more than worth the cost of years of study and experimentation. That cost, however—most of which was borne by foundations and universities, but much of it by hospitals—was reflected in the skyrocketing costs of medical care. Few Americans could afford even a brief period of hospitalization, and even with help from insurance plans (such as Blue Cross), many people were still unable to pay. The aged were especially hard hit, and, despite opposition from the American Medical Association, Congress passed a Medicare bill, which went into effect in 1966. Administrated through Social Security, Medicare provided most hospitalization costs for citizens over sixty-five. An additional voluntary program helped with doctor bills.

Education, always a field in which Americans have had strong opinions, was in great ferment during the post-

The University of Minnesota, with more than 40,000 students on three campuses, is, like all American universities, hard put to find places for its many applicants.

war years, and especially after the first Soviet Sputnik went up in 1957. To help the educators Congress, in 1958 passed the National Defense Education Act providing federal help for science teaching and equipment. Gradually concern arose over the relative neglect of the humanities and the liberal arts, and in the '60s there was additional effort—through college fund-raising drives and foundation grants—to maintain excellence in the liberal arts curricula. A measure of the rising interest in education, both because of the Sputniks and because of society's demand for greater skills, was the increase in the amount of time Americans spent in school. Among adults over 25, the median of formal schooling rose from 9.3 years in 1950 to 10.6 in 1960. Colleges enrolled about 15% of the college-age population in 1940; by 1963 they had 40% of it.

Despite its triumphs, many critics thought that America verged dangerously toward mediocre sameness and conformity. They argued that Americans watched the same television programs, read the same syndicated columnists and obtained their news through the same wire services.

But others pointed out that these critics overlooked some developments that might be called a cultural explosion. There was a proliferation of local symphony orchestras and theater groups, drawing mostly on home talent. The summer-theater movement brought professional casts within the reach and pocketbook of millions of Americans who had little opportunity to visit Broadway. Sales of books boomed under the impetus of book clubs and inexpensive paperbacks. Records sold in vast quantities, especially after the development of high-fidelity and stereophonic equipment.

During the Kennedy years, artists received special attention and became an important part of Washington's "inner circle." The President's Commission on the Fine Arts was established, with painter William Walton at its head, and plans were made to form a National Center for the Performing Arts. After Kennedy's death planning was continued, and the Arts Center will bear his name.

Civil rights

A century had passed since the Civil War was fought over the position of the Negro in American life and since adoption of the Constitutional amendments designed to assure him the rights of other citizens—the Thirteenth, abolishing slavery; the Fourteenth, assuring each person "the equal protection of the laws"; and the Fifteenth, declaring that "the right of citizens . . . to vote shall not be denied or abridged . . . on account of race, color, or previous condition of servitude." Yet throughout much of the South, the Negro had been only a second-class citizen—kept from voting by pressures and obstructive regulations, sent to segregated schools, and required to remain separate from whites in many public places.

These matters had long troubled the consciences of many Americans. In a time of cold war, however, segregation became an acute embarrassment to the country, for the United States sought to depict itself as a true democracy when in fact millions of its citizens were denied their democratic rights. Americans found that segregation gave the country a bad reputation abroad, especially in the newly independent African nations.

Efforts to improve the lot of the Negro through legislation foundered repeatedly in the House and Senate. It was, therefore, from another direction that an effective assault on segregation had to come. It came in 1954 from the Supreme Court.

For many years, the doctrine of the court had been based on the decision in the case of *Plessy vs. Ferguson* in 1896. This upheld Louisiana's practice of providing "equal but separate accommodations for the white and colored races" in railway cars and other public places. In May, 1954, however, a unanimous court ruled in the case of *Brown vs. Board of Education* that the separate but equal concept had to give way. A year later, the court directed Southern school districts to proceed toward desegregation "with all deliberate speed."

In the years that followed, there was slow but steady progress toward racial integration of Southern schools, although it was marked by some spectacular conflicts. Notable among these was a collision between federal and state authority in Little Rock, Arkansas, in 1957. Pursuant to the Supreme Court decision, the Little Rock board of education had adopted a plan of integration that called for the admission of some Negroes to the city's Central High School, starting in September, 1957.

As the time for the opening of school approached, Governor Orval M. Faubus declared that integration would threaten the peace. He stationed National Guard units around the high school. When nine Negroes attempted to enroll, Faubus ordered the National Guard to bar them.

Under federal injunction, the National Guard was withdrawn. Then rioting mobs appeared, bent on keeping Negroes from the school. At that juncture, President Eisenhower ordered federal troops into the city and called the National Guard into federal service, thereby removing it from the governor's control. Under the protection of federal bayonets, the Negroes entered the school. The principle that the federal government would not tolerate local defiance of court orders on integration had been established.

There were some federal actions in behalf of civil rights besides those taken by the courts. The Eisenhower administration ordered an end to segregation in the armed services. In 1957, Congress passed the Civil Rights Act, the first significant legislation in the field since reconstruction. It created a Civil Rights Commission and gave the government new power to seek injunctions against interference with Negro voting.

Much of the impetus toward faster desegregation, however, came from the Negroes themselves, together with some supporting whites. In 1960, a group of Negro students entered a department store in Greensboro, North Carolina, and sat quietly at the lunch counter to protest the fact that Negroes were not served there. That was the beginning of the "sit-in" movement that spread quickly through the South and resulted in the desegregation of several lunch counters and waiting rooms. A year later, some Negro organizations started the practice of "freedom rides"—Negroes and whites riding through the South and entering "white" waiting rooms. Many of the sit-in demonstrators and freedom riders were arrested, but they succeeded in quickening the pace of desegregation.

But as the pace quickened, resistance in many parts of the country stiffened. In 1962 and 1963, the governors of both Alabama and Mississippi attempted to prevent Negroes from enrolling in their respective state universities and National Guard troops, activated by President Kennedy, had to be employed to quell violent riots. In Birmingham, Alabama, a protest march led by Rev. Martin Luther King, Jr., was interrupted by Police Commissioner Eugene "Bull" Connor, who unleashed a pack of police dogs on the marchers and jailed Dr. King. A church in Birmingham was bombed, killing and maiming Negro children. On the very night that President Kennedy, in a televised speech, called for a settlement of the "moral

The scenes of violence that took place in Little Rock (top), where paratroopers escort nine Negro pupils into a high school, and at the University of Mississippi (center), where federal troops quell rioting students who protested the admission of one Negro, were the result of the Supreme Court's 1954 decision that segregation in schools was illegal. Civil rights are now largely established by decisions of the court, which in early 1963 was (seated, left to right) Tom C. Clark, Hugo L. Black, Chief Justice Earl Warren, William O. Douglas, John M. Harlan; (standing) Byron R. White, William J. Brennan, Jr., Potter Stewart, and Arthur J. Goldberg.

ALL: UNITED PRESS INTERNATIONAL

issue" that racial injustice had become, Mississippi NAACP chief Medgar Evers was assassinated in Jackson.

On June 19, 1963, Kennedy sent the strongest civil rights bill in history to Congress. The bill called for a public accommodations section, which would make it illegal to discriminate in public facilities, granted the Attorney General authority to file suit where school desegregation had not been carried out, assured fair employment practices, and withheld federal funds from projects in which discrimination was practiced. When it became apparent that congressional action was not going to be as swift as had been hoped, Negro leaders announced plans for a march on Washington. Kennedy was apprehensive. If fewer than the estimated 100,000 marchers should show up, he reasoned, Congress might feel that passage of the bill was not urgent.

But in August, a quarter of a million black and white Americans converged on Washington, marched to the Lincoln Memorial, and heard Dr. King describe his dream "that on the red hills of Georgia the sons of former slaves and the sons of former slave-owners will be able to sit together at the table of brotherhood."

In July, 1964, the Civil Rights bill became law. President Kennedy's cause had become his memorial. The next year his successor, Lyndon Johnson, promoted passage of another rights bill, ensuring Negro voting rights in many areas where those rights had been denied. The bill passed in 1965, ending the period of legislative action. As older rights leaders began moving their activities into the courts, where the new laws could be effected, a number of younger men—such as Stokely Carmichael, the leader of the Student Nonviolent Coordinating Committee—remained skeptical of the government's willingness to act in behalf of minority rights. They sought to achieve "black power" through political means within the Negro community alone.

The anti-poverty program

Shortly before his death, President Kennedy remarked that "the time has come to organize a national assault on the causes of poverty, a comprehensive program, across the board." President Johnson also believed that the existence of poverty-pockets in the coal regions and hill country and big cities of the richest nation in the world was absurd and unnecessary.

In the summer of 1964, the Office of Economic Opportunity was established. Through this office, federal funds were provided for such organizations as VISTA (Volunteers in Service to America—the domestic Peace Corps), the Job Corps (for training unemployed young citizens), the Neighborhood Youth Corps, and to other groups that provided assistance for migrant workers, adult education, and loans to farmers and small businessmen. In all, about 2.3 billion dollars were allocated during the first

WIDE WORLD

Besides fogging the skylines of New York (above) and other American cities, air pollution (known as smog) became a serious health hazard to Americans during the 1950s and 1960s.

two years. The poverty program was critized for mistakes, and funds were reduced because of the costs of the war in Vietnam. But there were successes, such as Head Start, which provided education for underprivileged pre-school children in order to help compensate for their deprived environment.

The cities

By 1920, at least half the population of the United States lived in towns and cities. The trend toward urbanization hit a peak in the two decades following World War II; by 1965, 7 out of 10 Americans lived in metropolitan areas. Ironically, in those same twenty years, the populations of most big cities remained the same and in many cases shrank. The explanation lies in the fact that most metropolitan growth has centered on the suburbs.

By the end of the 1950s the suburbs of America had grown so large that the environs of one city often reached those of another. The result was a phenomenon called megalopolis—a huge, sprawling area of urban or near-urban population density. The most highly developed megalopolis stretched from Washington, D.C. to Boston and included Baltimore, Wilmington, Philadelphia, Newark-Trenton, New York, Hartford, and Providence. Others were developing between San Francisco and San Diego in California and between the large cities situated on the Great Lakes.

In 1967, megalopoleis contained 20

per cent of America's people—on less than 1½ per cent of America's land. Since they were not, despite their common problems, administered by a single agency, their problems were almost impossible to handle.

The problems were frustratingly cyclic. Suburban growth demanded more highways; more highways tended to stimulate further suburban development; further development demanded more highways; the highways converged on the city, creating a more or less permanent congestion problem. And the slow-moving automobiles, spitting their carbon exhausts into the air, polluted it. By 1970 the atmosphere was expected to contain about 200 million tons of pollutants. It is not certain what constitutes unbreathable air; but pulmonary emphysema, a once-rare respiratory disorder that occurs in direct correlation to the level of pollution, has been responsible since the mid-1960s for the disabling and death of more American men than any other illness except heart disease.

Meanwhile, the permanent traffic congestion and the miserable air made city living more and more difficult to tolerate. So more people of the middle class left.

The departure of the middle class from the cities created a vacuum that drove still more middle class families from town. After the war, the old immigrants were replaced by Negroes, Puerto Ricans, and whites from the Southern backwoods and hills. Victims of discrimination and inadequate education, the newcomers formed the hard core of the city's unemployed. Slum areas where unemployment was high tended to be breeding grounds for crime, and the urban crime rate in the 1960s climbed.

The suburban middle class continued to earn its living in the city, but spent its money outside and paid taxes outside. The city, losing important revenue, had no choice but to increase its own taxes and reduce its services.

For the people left behind—the poor—the city became a virtual prison. Unprepared in the special skills needed in the urban-industrial age, they found even the market for unskilled labor diminished. (Automatic elevators, for example, eliminated hundreds of thousands of jobs.)

To make matters worse for the urban poor, the wealth of American society was revealed to them constantly. Television, a fixture in the American home since the 1950s, advertised the lavish products of American industry, documented huge government expenditures abroad, reported in matter-of-fact tones the billions of dollars being exchanged from day to day in the financial world, and showed prosperous American families in well-furnished, spacious apartments and homes. No poor people were ever before so consistently reminded of what they were missing.

For a while—especially after the civil rights bills of 1964 and 1965—progress seemed imminent. But judi-

Taking cover behind parked cars, police, National Guardsmen, and Army paratroopers seek out snipers in this residential neighborhood of Detroit during the terrible riots of 1967.

cial processes necessary to effect the legislation were slow, and the poverty program was new and required much trial and error. Discrimination had not been—and could not be—legislated away.

The frustations began to come to a head in 1966. Angered by the speeches of "black power" advocates, and involved with the war in Vietnam, Congress defeated a new civil rights bill submitted by the administration. In 1967 funds for the poverty program were substantially cut, and the whole program seemed in trouble. In July a federal rat-extermination appropriation was literally laughed off by congressional leaders and defeated.

Riots in urban ghettos had become an unfortunate part of the American summertime scene in the sixties. In 1967 they hit a peak. After a Negro taxicab driver was arrested in Newark, New Jersey, false rumors of his having been beaten to death by police were circulated. Negroes began stoning the police precinct in which the driver was housed, the mob spirit caught on, and the ghetto's stores were broken into, looted, and often set aflame. Police and National Guardsmen moved in and a curfew was declared, but the looting and shooting continued. For five days arson and sniping were the rule, the fires of frustration and race-hatred more often fanned than extinguished by ill-prepared and sometimes trigger-happy police and guardsmen. Riots on a smaller scale broke out in Plainfield, (New Jersey), Omaha, Chicago, Tampa, Cincinnati, Atlanta, Cambridge, Maryland, Kansas City, Buffalo, Minneapolis, and New York. Newark, however, seemed to be the hardest hit. Then Detroit—the city widely thought of as one of the most progressive in the North with regard to Negro-white relations, a city with no sharply defined "black belt" and with good job opportunities—exploded. On a window-breaking, looting, fire-setting spree unparalleled in American history, young Negroes gutted miles of Detroit, making parts of the city look like a bombed out Dresden or Tokyo of World War II. The liquor, high-fidelity sets, televisions, washing machines, bicycles, cameras, and gas ranges, taken from the stores by looters, resembled, as one sociologist observed, "a singing commercial for all the things they had seen on television."

With the help of United States Army paratroopers, the uprising was finally put down. Forty people were dead, more than two thousand were injured, and over four thousand were under arrest; the damage to Detroit was estimated at a half-billion dollars. Worst of all, there seemed no adequate explanation for why the riots had begun.

As the center of the riot scene shifted from Detroit to Milwaukee, President Johnson formed a commission to investigate the tragedy and recommend programs to prevent its repetition. Congressional leaders had many and varied explanations. Black power advocates called for violent overthrow of the government and urged Negroes to "burn America down." Politicians played politics with the situation, while most Americans reacted with mixtures of anger, fear, grief. The only thing nobody had was a solution.

But the picture was not entirely gloomy. At various levels of government, officials had expressed an awareness that drastic administrative changes had to be made before the essential problems of the city could be rooted out. At the federal level the Department of Housing and Urban Development and the Department of Transportation had been formed within the executive branch. Through such organizations, the common problems of megalopoleis could be attacked and properly coordinated. Local officials had begun forming multicity and multistate authorities to deal with air and water pollution and other problems.

The problems still exist, but the American people are aware of them and appear anxious to do something about them. The future will be the biggest challenge to what the world has come to know as "American know-how."

FOR FURTHER READING

Agar, Herbert. *Price of Power: America Since 1945.* Chicago: University of Chicago, 1957. A brief survey of America's emergence into world leadership in the decade after World War II. Highly readable.

Caidin, Martin. *Rendezvous in Space: The Story of Projects Mercury, Gemini, Dyna-Soar and Apollo.* New York: Dutton, 1962. A recent commentary on America's progress in space exploration.

Donovan, Robert J. *Eisenhower: The Inside Story.* New York: Harpers, 1956. An objective report of Eisenhower's first three years in office, by a newspaperman with access to White House papers.

Evans, Rowland, and Novak, Robert. *Lyndon B. Johnson: The Exercise of Power.* New York: The New American Library, Inc., 1966. An objective look at the career of the thirty-sixth President.

Goldwater, Barry. *Conscience of a Conservative.* New York: Macfadden (paperback), 1960. A prominent Senator presents the conservative political viewpoint.

Graebner, Norman A. *Cold War Diplomacy, 1945–1960.* New York: Anvil Books (paperback), 1962. A brief review of cold-war tensions.

Hillman, William. *Mr. President.* New York: Farrar, Straus, 1952. A well-illustrated and readable account of the Truman administration, with much family background.

Johnson, Walter. *1600 Pennsylvania Avenue.* Boston: Little, Brown, 1960. Deals with the Presidency from 1929 to 1959.

Kennan, George F. *Russia and the West.* Boston: Little, Brown, 1961. The former ambassador to Russia presents a historical and philosophical background to that country's relationship with the free world.

Leckie, Robert. *Conflict: The History of the Korean War.* New York: Putnam, 1962. A meticulously documented, full-scale account of the war in all its military, political, and human aspects, by a journalist and former marine.

Lubell, Samuel. *Revolt of the Moderates.* New York: Harper, 1956. An analysis by a shrewd political commentator of the realignment of national political forces that made possible the Eisenhower administration.

Rovere, Richard. *Senator Joe McCarthy.* New York: Harcourt, Brace, 1959. A journalistic portrait of a controversial public figure.

Schlesinger, Arthur M., Jr. *A Thousand Days.* Boston: Houghton Mifflin Co., 1965. An engrossing close-up of John F. Kennedy's Presidency, written by the eminent historian.

Spanier, John W. *American Foreign Policy Since World War II.* New York: Praeger, 1960. A study of how the cold war has affected American foreign policy.

White, Theodore H. *The Making of the President, 1960,* New York: Pocket Books (paperback), 1961, and *The Making of the President, 1964,* New York: Signet (paperback), 1966. Fascinating accounts of two Presidential elections.

ACKNOWLEDGMENTS

The editors are especially grateful to the following individuals and organizations for their generous assistance, and for their cooperation in making available pictorial materials from their collections:

Barbara Tyler, *Amon Carter Museum of Western Art;* Elizabeth P. Riegel, *Boston Museum of Fine Arts;* Marvin D. Schwartz, *Brooklyn Museum;* Mrs. Paul M. Rhymer, *Chicago Historical Society; Department of the Air Force; Department of the Army; Department of Defense; Department of the Navy;* Herbert E. Kahler, *Eastern National Park & Monument Association;* Elizabeth B. Drewry, Raymond Corry, William F. Stickle, *Franklin D. Roosevelt Library;* Clarence Hornung; Gail Black, *Isabella Stewart Gardner Museum;* Joseph J. Alvin, *Leach Corporation;* Edgar D. Breitenbach, Carl E. Stange, Virginia Daiker, *Library of Congress;* James Humphry, *Metropolitan Museum of Art;* Eugene D. Becker, *Minnesota Historical Society;* Pearl L. Moeller, *Museum of Modern Art;* Albert K. Baragwanath, *Museum of the City of New York; National Aeronautics & Space Administration;* Huntington Cairns, *National Gallery of Art;* Arthur B. Carlson, Paul Bride, *New York Historical Society;* Marion Wiethorn, Louise Leak, *New York Public Library;* Edgar M. Howell, *Division of Military History, Smithsonian Institution;* William B. Osgood, *State Street Bank and Trust Company;* Dean Krakel, *Thomas Gilcrease Institute of American History and Art;* Captain Wade DeWeese, *U.S. Naval Academy Museum;* Mrs. Ulrich Troubetzkoy, *Virginia Cavalcade;* Richard E. Kuehne, *West Point Museum;* Harold McCracken, *Whitney Gallery of Western Art;* Edward Bryant, *Whitney Museum of American Art;* Caroline Rollins, *Yale University Art Gallery.*

THE PRESIDENTS AND THE

ELECTION YEAR	PRESIDENT	PARTY	ELECTORAL VOTE
1788	**George Washington**		69
1792	**George Washington**		132
1796	**John Adams**	Federalist	71
1800	**Thomas Jefferson**	Democratic–Republican	73
1804	**Thomas Jefferson**	Democratic–Republican	162
1808	**James Madison**	Democratic–Republican	122
1812	**James Madison**	Democratic–Republican	128
1816	**James Monroe**	Democratic–Republican	183
1820	**James Monroe**	Democratic–Republican	231
1824	**John Quincy Adams**[1]	National Republican	84
1828	**Andrew Jackson**	Democratic	178
1832	**Andrew Jackson**	Democratic	219
1836	**Martin Van Buren**	Democratic	170
1840	**William Henry Harrison**	Whig	234
	John Tyler*	Whig	
1844	**James K. Polk**	Democratic	170
1848	**Zachary Taylor**	Whig	163
	Millard Fillmore*	Whig	
1852	**Franklin Pierce**	Democratic	254
1856	**James Buchanan**	Democratic	174
1860	**Abraham Lincoln**	Republican	180
1864	**Abraham Lincoln**	Republican	212
	Andrew Johnson*	Republican	
1868	**Ulysses S. Grant**	Republican	214
1872	**Ulysses S. Grant**	Republican	286
1876	**Rutherford B. Hayes**	Republican	185
1880	**James A. Garfield**	Republican	214
	Chester A. Arthur*	Republican	
1884	**Grover Cleveland**	Democratic	219
1888	**Benjamin Harrison**	Republican	233
1892	**Grover Cleveland**	Democratic	277
1896	**William McKinley**	Republican	271
1900	**William McKinley**	Republican	292
	Theodore Roosevelt*	Republican	
1904	**Theodore Roosevelt**	Republican	336
1908	**William H. Taft**	Republican	321
1912	**Woodrow Wilson**	Democratic	435
1916	**Woodrow Wilson**	Democratic	277
1920	**Warren G. Harding**	Republican	404
	Calvin Coolidge*	Republican	
1924	**Calvin Coolidge**	Republican	382
1928	**Herbert Hoover**	Republican	444
1932	**Franklin D. Roosevelt**	Democratic	472
1936	**Franklin D. Roosevelt**	Democratic	523
1940	**Franklin D. Roosevelt**	Democratic	449
1944	**Franklin D. Roosevelt**	Democratic	432
	Harry S. Truman*	Democratic	
1948	**Harry S. Truman**	Democratic	303
1952	**Dwight D. Eisenhower**	Republican	442
1956	**Dwight D. Eisenhower**	Republican	457
1960	**John F. Kennedy**	Democratic	303
	Lyndon B. Johnson*	Democratic	
1964	**Lyndon B. Johnson**	Democratic	486

*Vice-President who succeeded to the office of the elected President and completed his term.

[1]No one of the four candidates received a majority of the electoral votes, so the House of Representatives decided the election.

PRESIDENTIAL ELECTIONS

PRINCIPAL OPPONENT	PARTY	ELECTORAL VOTE	NUMBER OF STATES
(No opponent)			11
(No opponent)			15
Thomas Jefferson	Democratic–Republican	68	16
John Adams	Federalist	65	16
C. C. Pinckney	Federalist	14	17
C. C. Pinckney	Federalist	47	17
DeWitt Clinton	Federalist	89	18
Rufus King	Federalist	34	19
(No opponent)			24
Andrew Jackson	Democratic	99	24
John Quincy Adams	National Republican	83	24
Henry Clay	Whig	49	25
William H. Harrison	Whig	73	26
Martin Van Buren	Democratic	60	26
Henry Clay	Whig	105	26
Lewis Cass	Democratic	127	30
Winfield Scott	Whig	42	31
John C. Fremont	Republican	114	31
John C. Breckenridge	Democratic	72	33
George B. McClellan	Democratic	21	36
Horatio Seymour	Democratic	80	37
Horace Greeley[2]	Liberal Republican–Democratic		37
Samuel J. Tilden	Democratic	184	38
Winfield S. Hancock	Democratic	155	38
James G. Blaine	Republican	182	38
Grover Cleveland	Democratic	168	38
Benjamin Harrison	Republican	145	44
William J. Bryan	Democratic	176	45
William J. Bryan	Democratic	155	45
Alton B. Parker	Democratic	140	45
William J. Bryan	Democratic	162	46
Theodore Roosevelt	Progressive	88	48
Charles E. Hughes	Republican	254	48
James M. Cox	Democratic	127	48
John W. Davis	Democratic	136	48
Alfred E. Smith	Democratic	87	48
Herbert Hoover	Republican	59	48
Alfred M. Landon	Republican	8	48
Wendell L. Willkie	Republican	82	48
Thomas E. Dewey	Republican	99	48
Thomas E. Dewey	Republican	189	48
Adlai E. Stevenson	Democratic	89	48
Adlai E. Stevenson	Democratic	73	48
Richard M. Nixon	Republican	219	50
Barry M. Goldwater	Republican	52	50

[2] Because of Greeley's death before the electoral college met, the electors representing those who had voted for him cast their votes for other candidates.

THE PRESIDENTS AND THEIR CABINETS

PRESIDENT AND VICE-PRESIDENT	SECRETARY OF STATE	SECRETARY OF THE TREASURY	SECRETARY OF WAR
George Washington–John Adams 1789	Thomas Jefferson . . 1789 Edmund Randolph . 1794 Timothy Pickering . 1795	Alex. Hamilton . . . . 1789 Oliver Wolcott 1795	Henry Knox . . . . 1789 Timothy Pickering . 1795 James McHenry . . . 1796
John Adams–Thomas Jefferson 1797	Timothy Pickering . 1797 John Marshall 1800	Oliver Wolcott . . . . . 1797 Samuel Dexter 1801	James McHenry . . . 1797 John Marshall . . . . . 1800 Samuel Dexter . . . . . 1800 Roger Griswold 1801
Thomas Jefferson–Aaron Burr . . . . 1801 George Clinton 1805	James Madison 1801	Samuel Dexter . . . . . 1801 Albert Gallatin 1801	Henry Dearborn . . . 1801
James Madison–George Clinton . . . . 1809 Elbridge Gerry 1813	Robert Smith . . . . . . 1809 James Monroe 1811	Albert Gallatin . . . . 1809 G. W. Campbell . . . 1814 A. J. Dallas . . . . 1814 Wm. H. Crawford . . 1816	William Eustis . . . . . 1809 John Armstrong . . . 1813 James Monroe . . . . . 1814 Wm. H. Crawford . . 1815
James Monroe–Daniel D. Tompkins 1817	John Q. Adams 1817	Wm. H. Crawford . . 1817	Isaac Shelby . . . . 1817 George Graham . . . 1817 John C. Calhoun . . . 1817
John Quincy Adams–John C. Calhoun 1825	Henry Clay 1825	Richard Rush 1825	James Barbour . . . . . 1825 Peter B. Porter 1828
Andrew Jackson–John C. Calhoun . . . . 1829 Martin Van Buren 1833	Martin Van Buren . . 1829 Edward Livingston . 1831 Louis McLane . . . . . 1833 John Forsyth 1834	Samuel D. Ingham . 1829 Louis McLane . . . . . 1831 William J. Duane . . 1833 Roger B. Taney . . . . 1833 Levi Woodbury 1834	John H. Eaton . . . . . 1829 Lewis Cass . . . . 1831 Benjamin F. Butler . 1837
Martin Van Buren–Richard M. Johnson 1837	John Forsyth 1837	Levi Woodbury 1837	Joel R. Poinsett 1837
William H. Harrison–John Tyler 1841	Daniel Webster 1841	Thomas Ewing 1841	John Bell 1841
John Tyler 1841	Daniel Webster . . . . 1841 Hugh S. Legare . . . . 1843 Abel P. Upshur . . . . 1843 John C. Calhoun . . . 1844	Thomas Ewing . . . . . 1841 Walter Forward . . . . 1841 John C. Spencer . . . . 1843 George M. Bibb 1844	John Bell . . . . 1841 John McLean . . . . . . 1841 John C. Spencer . . . . 1841 James M. Porter . . . 1843 William Wilkins . . . 1844
James K. Polk–George M. Dallas 1845	James Buchanan . . . 1845	Robert J. Walker . . . 1845	William L. Marcy . . 1845
Zachary Taylor–Millard Fillmore 1849	John M. Clayton . . . 1849	Wm. M. Meredith . . 1849	Geo. W. Crawford . 1849
Millard Fillmore 1850	Daniel Webster . . . . 1850 Edward Everett 1852	Thomas Corwin 1850	Charles M. Conrad . 1850
Franklin Pierce–William R. King 1853	William L. Marcy . . 1853	James Guthrie 1853	Jefferson Davis 1853
James Buchanan–John C. Breckinridge 1857	Lewis Cass . . . . 1857 Jeremiah S. Black . . 1860	Howell Cobb . . . . . . 1857 Philip F. Thomas . . . 1860 John A. Dix 1861	John B. Floyd . . . . . 1857 Joseph Holt 1861
Abraham Lincoln–Hannibal Hamlin . . . . 1861 Andrew Johnson 1865	William H. Seward . 1861	Salmon P. Chase . . . 1861 Wm. P. Fessenden . . 1864 Hugh McCulloch . . 1865	Simon Cameron . . . 1861 Edwin M. Stanton . . 1862
Andrew Johnson 1865	William H. Seward . 1865	Hugh McCulloch . . 1865	Edwin M. Stanton . . 1865 Ulysses S. Grant . . . 1867 Lorenzo Thomas . . . 1868 John M. Schofield . . 1868

SECRETARY OF THE NAVY	SECRETARY OF THE INTERIOR	POSTMASTER GENERAL	ATTORNEY GENERAL
	Established March 3, 1849	Samuel Osgood .... 1789 Timothy Pickering . 1791 Joseph Habersham . 1795	Edmund Randolph . 1789 William Bradford .. 1794 Charles Lee 1795
Benjamin Stoddert.. 1798		Joseph Habersham . 1797	Charles Lee .... 1797 Theophilus Parsons. 1801
Benjamin Stoddert.. 1801 Robert Smith ...... 1801 J. Crowninshield ... 1805		Joseph Habersham . 1801 Gideon Granger ... 1801	Levi Lincoln....... 1801 Robert Smith...... 1805 John Breckinridge.. 1805 Caesar A. Rodney.. 1807
Paul Hamilton..... 1809 William Jones ..... 1813 B.W.Crowninshield 1814		Gideon Granger ... 1809 Return J. Meigs, Jr.. 1814	Caesar A. Rodney.. 1809 William Pinckney .. 1811 Richard Rush 1814
B.W.Crowninshield 1817 Smith Thompson... 1818 S. L. Southard 1823		Return J. Meigs, Jr.. 1817 John McLean...... 1823	Richard Rush ..... 1817 William Wirt 1817
S. L. Southard 1825		John McLean...... 1825	William Wirt 1825
John Branch....... 1829 Levi Woodbury .... 1831 Mahlon Dickerson . 1834		William T. Barry... 1829 Amos Kendall 1835	John M. Berrien ... 1829 Roger B. Taney .... 1831 Benjamin F. Butler . 1833
Mahlon Dickerson . 1837 James K. Paulding.. 1838		Amos Kendall ..... 1837 John M. Niles 1840	Benjamin F. Butler . 1837 Felix Grundy...... 1838 Henry D. Gilpin ... 1840
George E. Badger .. 1841		Francis Granger ... 1841	John J. Crittenden.. 1841
George E. Badger .. 1841 Abel P. Upshur .... 1841 David Henshaw.... 1843 Thomas W. Gilmer . 1844 John Y. Mason 1844		Francis Granger ... 1841 Chas. A. Wickliffe.. 1841	John J. Crittenden.. 1841 Hugh S. Legare .... 1841 John Nelson....... 1843
George Bancroft ... 1845 John Y. Mason 1846		Cave Johnson 1845	John Y. Mason .... 1845 Nathan Clifford.... 1846 Isaac Toucey 1848
William B. Preston . 1849	Thomas Ewing..... 1849	Jacob Collamer 1849	Reverdy Johnson... 1849
Wm. A. Graham ... 1850 John P. Kennedy ... 1852	Alex. H. H. Stuart.. 1850	Nathan K. Hall .... 1850 Sam. D. Hubbard .. 1852	John J. Crittenden.. 1850
James C. Dobbin... 1853	Robert McClelland. 1853	James Campbell ... 1853	Caleb Cushing..... 1853
Isaac Toucey 1857	Jacob Thompson... 1857	Aaron V. Brown ... 1857 Joseph Holt 1859	Jeremiah S. Black .. 1857 Edwin M. Stanton.. 1860
Gideon Welles 1861	Caleb B. Smith..... 1861 John P. Usher 1863	Horatio King...... 1861 Montgomery Blair . 1861 William Dennison.. 1864	Edward Bates...... 1861 Titian J. Coffey .... 1863 James Speed...... 1864
Gideon Welles 1865	John P. Usher ..... 1865 James Harlan...... 1865 O. H. Browning.... 1866	William Dennison.. 1865 Alex. W. Randall... 1866	James Speed....... 1865 Henry Stanbery.... 1866 William M. Evarts.. 1868

OTHER MEMBERS
SECRETARY OF AGRICULTURE
Established February 11, 1889
Norman J. Colman .... 1889 Jeremiah M. Rusk..... 1889 J. Sterling Morton..... 1893 James Wilson......... 1897 James Wilson......... 1901 James Wilson......... 1909 David F. Houston..... 1913 Edward T. Meredith ... 1920 Henry C. Wallace ..... 1921 Howard M. Gore...... 1924 William M. Jardine.... 1925 Arthur M. Hyde....... 1929 Henry A. Wallace ..... 1933 Claude R. Wickard .... 1940 Clinton P. Anderson ... 1945 Charles F. Brannan.... 1948 Ezra Taft Benson...... 1953 Orville L. Freeman 1961
SECRETARY OF COMMERCE AND LABOR
Established February 14, 1903
George B. Cortelyou ... 1903 Victor H. Metcalf...... 1904 Oscar S. Straus........ 1906 Charles Nagel......... 1909
SECRETARY OF COMMERCE†
William C. Redfield.... 1913 Joshua W. Alexander .. 1919 Herbert Hoover....... 1921 Herbert Hoover....... 1925 William F. Whiting.... 1928 Robert P. Lamont..... 1929 Roy D. Chapin........ 1932 Daniel C. Roper....... 1933 Harry L. Hopkins ..... 1939 Jesse Jones .... 1940 Henry A. Wallace..... 1945 W. A. Harriman ...... 1946 Charles Sawyer .... 1948 Sinclair Weeks........ 1953 Luther Hodges........ 1961 John T. Connor....... 1965 Alexander Trowbridge............ 1967

PRESIDENT AND VICE-PRESIDENT	SECRETARY OF STATE	SECRETARY OF THE TREASURY	SECRETARY OF WAR
Ulysses S. Grant–Schuyler Colfax . . . 1869 Henry Wilson . . . 1873	E. B. Washburne . . . 1869 Hamilton Fish . . . 1869	George S. Boutwell . 1869 W. A. Richardson . . 1873 Benj. H. Bristow . . . 1874 Lot M. Morrill. . . . 1876	John A. Rawlins . . . 1869 W. T. Sherman . . . . 1869 Wm. W. Belknap . . . 1869 Alphonso Taft . . . . 1876 James D. Cameron . 1876
Rutherford B. Hayes–William A. Wheeler . . . 1877	William M. Evarts . 1877	John Sherman 1877	Geo. W. McCrary . . 1877 Alexander Ramsey . 1879
James A. Garfield–Chester A. Arthur . . . 1881	James G. Blaine. . . . 1881	William Windom. . . 1881	Robert T. Lincoln . . 1881
Chester A. Arthur . . . 1881	Frederick T. Freling-huysen . . . 1881	Charles J. Folger . . . 1881 Walter Q. Gresham . 1884 Hugh McCulloch . . 1884	Robert T. Lincoln . . 1881
Grover Cleveland–Thomas A. Hendricks . . . 1885	Thomas F. Bayard . 1885	Daniel Manning . . . 1885 Chas. S. Fairchild . . 1887	Wm. C. Endicott . . . 1885
Benjamin Harrison–Levi P. Morton . . . 1889	James G. Blaine. . . . 1889 John W. Foster 1892	William Windom. . . 1889 Charles Foster 1891	Redfield Proctor . . . 1889 Stephen B. Elkins . . 1891
Grover Cleveland–Adlai E. Stevenson . . . 1893	Walter Q. Gresham . 1893 Richard Olney 1895	John G. Carlisle . . . 1893	Daniel S. Lamont . . 1893
William McKinley–Garret A. Hobart . . . 1897 Theodore Roosevelt . . . 1901	John Sherman . . . . . 1897 William R. Day . . . . 1897 John Hay 1898	Lyman J. Gage 1897	Russell A. Alger . . . 1897 Elihu Root 1899
Theodore Roosevelt . . . 1901 Charles W. Fairbanks . . . 1905	John Hay . . . . 1901 Elihu Root . . . . 1905 Robert Bacon 1909	Lyman J. Gage . . . . 1901 Leslie M. Shaw . . . . 1902 Geo. B. Cortelyou . . 1907	Elihu Root . . . . 1901 William H. Taft . . . . 1904 Luke E. Wright 1908
William H. Taft–James S. Sherman . . . 1909	Philander C. Knox . 1909	Fkln. MacVeagh . . . 1909	J. M. Dickinson . . . . 1909 Henry L. Stimson . . 1911
Woodrow Wilson–Thomas R. Marshall . . . 1913	William J. Bryan . . . 1913 Robert Lansing . . . . 1915 Bainbridge Colby . . 1920	Wm. G. McAdoo . . 1913 Carter Glass. . . . . . . 1919 David F. Houston . . 1929	L. M. Garrison . . . . 1913 Newton D. Baker . . 1916
Warren G. Harding–Calvin Coolidge . . . 1921	Charles E. Hughes. . 1921	Andrew W. Mellon . 1921	John W. Weeks 1921
Calvin Coolidge . . . 1923 Charles G. Dawes . . . 1925	Charles E. Hughes. . 1923 Frank B. Kellogg. . . 1925	Andrew W. Mellon . 1923	John W. Weeks . . . . 1923 Dwight F. Davis . . . 1925
Herbert C. Hoover–Charles Curtis . . . 1929	Henry L. Stimson . . 1929	Andrew W. Mellon . 1929 Ogden L. Mills. 1932	James W. Good . . . . 1929 Patrick J. Hurley . . . 1929
Franklin Delano Roosevelt–John Nance Garner . . . 1933 Henry A. Wallace . . . 1941 Harry S. Truman . . . 1945	Cordell Hull. . . . . . . 1933 Edward R. Stettinius, Jr. . . . 1944	Wm. H. Woodin . . . 1933 Henry Morgenthau, Jr. . . . 1934	George H. Dern. . . . 1933 H. A. Woodring . . . 1936 Henry L. Stimson . . 1940
Harry S. Truman . . . 1945 Alben W. Barkley . . . 1949	James F. Byrnes. . . . 1945 Geo. C. Marshall . . 1947 Dean Acheson 1949	Fred M. Vinson . . . . 1945 John W. Snyder 1946	Robt. P. Patterson. . 1945 Ken. C. Royall. . . . 1947*
Dwight D. Eisenhower–Richard M. Nixon . . . 1953	John F. Dulles . . . . . 1953 Christian A. Herter . 1959	G. M. Humphrey . . 1953 Robt. B. Anderson . 1957	
John F. Kennedy–Lyndon B. Johnson . . . 1961	Dean Rusk 1961	C. Douglas Dillon . . 1961	
Lyndon B. Johnson . . . 1963 Hubert H. Humphrey . . . 1965	Dean Rusk 1963	C. Douglas Dillon . . 1963 Henry H. Fowler . . . 1965	

*On July 26, 1947, the Department of War and the Department of the Navy were combined into a newly established Department of Defense.

SECRETARY OF THE NAVY	SECRETARY OF THE INTERIOR	POSTMASTER GENERAL	ATTORNEY GENERAL
Adolph E. Borie. . . . 1869 Geo. M. Robeson . . 1869	Jacob D. Cox. . . . . . 1869 Columbus Delano . . 1870 Zach. Chandler 1875	John A. J. Creswell . 1869 James W. Marshall . 1874 Marshall Jewell . . . . 1874 James N. Tyner 1876	Ebenezer R. Hoar . . 1869 Amos T. Ackerman. 1870 Geo. H. Williams . . 1871 Edw. Pierrepont . . . 1875 Alphonso Taft 1876
R. W. Thompson . . . 1877 Nathan Goff, Jr. . . . 1881	Carl Schurz 1877	David M. Key . . . . . 1877 Horace Maynard . . . 1880	Charles Devens 1877
William H. Hunt . . . 1881	Sam. J. Kirkwood . . 1881	Thomas L. James . . 1881	Wayne MacVeagh . . 1881
Wm. E. Chandler. . . 1881	Henry M. Teller. . . . 1881	Timothy O. Howe . . 1881 Walter Q. Gresham. 1883 Frank Hatton 1884	Benj. H. Brewster . . 1881
William C. Whitney 1885	L. Q. C. Lamar . . . . 1885 William F. Vilas . . . 1888	William F. Vilas . . . 1885 Don M. Dickinson . 1888	A. H. Garland 1885
Benjamin F. Tracy. . 1889	John W. Noble 1889	John Wanamaker . . 1889	Wm. H. H. Miller . . 1889
Hilary A. Herbert . . 1893	Hoke Smith . . . . 1893 David R. Francis. . . 1896	Wilson S. Bissell . . . 1893 William L. Wilson. . 1895	Richard Olney . . . . . 1893 Judson Harmon. . . . 1895
John D. Long. 1897	Cornelius N. Bliss . . 1897 E. A. Hitchcock. . . . 1899	James A. Gary. . . . . 1897 Charles E. Smith . . . 1898	Joseph McKenna. . . 1897 John W. Griggs . . . . 1897 Philander C. Knox . 1901
John D. Long. . . . . . 1901 William H. Moody . 1902 Paul Morton . . . . . . 1904 Chas. J. Bonaparte . 1905 Victor H. Metcalf . . 1907 T. H. Newberry 1908	E. A. Hitchcock. . . . 1901 James R. Garfield . . 1907	Charles E. Smith . . . 1901 Henry C. Payne . . . . 1902 Robert J. Wynne . . . 1904 Geo. B. Cortelyou . . 1905 Geo. von L. Meyer . 1907	Philander C. Knox . 1901 William H. Moody . 1904 Chas. J. Bonaparte . 1907
Geo. von L. Meyer . 1909	R. A. Ballinger . . . . 1909 Walter L. Fisher . . . 1911	F. H. Hitchcock. . . . 1909	G. W. Wickersham . 1909
Josephus Daniels . . . 1913	Franklin K. Lane . . 1913 John B. Payne 1920	Albert S. Burleson. . 1913	J. C. McReynolds . . 1913 Thos. W. Gregory . . 1914 A. Mitchell Palmer . 1919
Edwin Denby. 1921	Albert B. Fall. . . . . . 1921 Hubert Work. 1923	Will H. Hays . . . . . . 1921 Hubert Work . . . . . . 1922 Harry S. New. 1923	H. M. Daugherty. . . 1921
Edwin Denby . . . . . . 1923 Curtis D. Wilbur . . . 1924	Hubert Work . . . . . . 1923 Roy O. West 1928	Harry S. New. 1923	H. M Daugherty. . . 1923 Harlan F. Stone. . . . 1924 John G. Sargent. . . . 1925
Charles F. Adams . . 1929	Ray L. Wilbur 1929	Walter F. Brown . . . 1929	Wm. D. Mitchell . . . 1929
Claude A. Swanson . 1933 Charles Edison. . . . . 1940 Frank Knox 1940	Harold L. Ickes 1933	James A. Farley. . . . 1933 Frank C. Walker . . . 1940	H. S. Cummings . . . 1933 Frank Murphy. . . . . 1939 Robert H. Jackson . 1940 Francis Biddle 1941
James V. Forrestal. 1945*	Harold L. Ickes . . . . 1945 Julius C. Krug . . . . . 1946 Oscar L. Chapman . 1949	Frank C. Walker . . . 1945 Robt. E. Hannegan . 1945 J. M. Donaldson . . . 1947	Tom C. Clark. . . . . . 1945 J. H. McGrath. . . . . 1949 J. P. McGranery . . . 1952
	Douglas McKay . . . 1953 Fred A. Seaton 1956	A. E. Summerfield . . 1953	H. Brownell, Jr. . . . 1953 William P. Rogers . . 1957
	Stewart L. Udall . . . 1961	J. Edward Day . . . . 1961 John A. Gronouski. 1963	Robert F. Kennedy . 1961
	Stewart L. Udall . . . 1963	John A. Gronouski . 1963 Lawrence O'Brien . . 1965	Robert F. Kennedy . 1963 Nicholas Katzen- back . . . . 1964 W. Ramsey Clark . . 1967

OTHER MEMBERS

SECRETARY OF LABOR†

Established March 4, 1913

William B. Wilson 1913
James J. Davis 1921
James J. Davis 1923
James J. Davis 1929
William N. Doak 1930
Frances Perkins 1933
L. B. Schwellenbach . . . 1945
Maurice J. Tobin 1948
Martin P. Durkin. 1953
James P. Mitchell. 1953
Arthur J. Goldberg 1961
W. Willard Wirtz 1962

SECRETARY OF DEFENSE

Established July 26, 1947

James V. Forrestal 1947
Louis A. Johnson 1949
George C. Marshall 1950
Robert A. Lovett 1951
Charles E. Wilson 1953
Neil H. McElroy 1957
Thomas S. Gates, Jr. . . . 1959
Robert S. McNamara . . 1961

SECRETARY OF HEALTH, EDUCATION, AND WELFARE

Established April 1, 1953

Oveta Culp Hobby. 1953
Marion B. Folsom 1955
Arthur S. Flemming. . . . 1958
Abraham A. Ribicoff. . . 1961
Anthony J. Celebrezze . . 1962
John W. Gardner 1965

SECRETARY OF HOUSING AND URBAN DEVELOPMENT

Established September 9, 1965

Robert C. Weaver 1966

SECRETARY OF TRANSPORTATION

Established October 15, 1966

Alan S. Boyd 1967

†On March 4, 1913, the Department of Commerce and Labor was divided into the Department of Commerce and the Department of Labor.

INDEX

FOR ALL 16 VOLUMES

PAGE NUMBERS FOR EACH VOLUME

VOL. 1:	1-89	VOL. 5:	360–449	VOL. 9:	720–809	VOL. 13:	1080–1169
VOL. 2:	90–179	VOL. 6:	450–539	VOL. 10:	810–899	VOL. 14:	1170–1259
VOL. 3:	180–269	VOL. 7:	540–629	VOL. 11:	900–989	VOL. 15:	1260–1349
VOL. 4:	270–359	VOL. 8:	630–719	VOL. 12:	990–1079	VOL. 16:	1350–1439

Bold-face numerals indicate illustrations

A

B

C

PAGE NUMBERS FOR EACH VOLUME

VOL. 1:	1–89	VOL. 5:	360–449	VOL. 9:	720–809	VOL. 13:	1080–1169
VOL. 2:	90–179	VOL. 6:	450–539	VOL. 10:	810–899	VOL. 14:	1170–1259
VOL. 3:	180–269	VOL. 7:	540–629	VOL. 11:	900–989	VOL. 15:	1260–1349
VOL. 4:	270–359	VOL. 8:	630–719	VOL. 12:	990–1079	VOL. 16:	1350–1439

D

E

F

PAGE NUMBERS FOR EACH VOLUME

VOL. 1:	1–89	VOL. 5:	360–449	VOL. 9:	720–809	VOL. 13:	1080–1169
VOL. 2:	90–179	VOL. 6:	450–539	VOL. 10:	810–899	VOL. 14:	1170–1259
VOL. 3:	180–269	VOL. 7:	540–629	VOL. 11:	900–989	VOL. 15:	1260–1349
VOL. 4:	270–359	VOL. 8:	630–719	VOL. 12:	990–1079	VOL. 16:	1350–1439

G

H

PAGE NUMBERS FOR EACH VOLUME

VOL. 1:	1–89	VOL. 5:	360–449	VOL. 9:	720–809	VOL. 13:	1080–1169
VOL. 2:	90–179	VOL. 6:	450–539	VOL. 10:	810–899	VOL. 14:	1170–1259
VOL. 3:	180–269	VOL. 7:	540–629	VOL. 11:	900–989	VOL. 15:	1260–1349
VOL. 4:	270–359	VOL. 8:	630–719	VOL. 12:	990–1079	VOL. 16:	1350–1439

I

J

K

L

M

PAGE NUMBERS FOR EACH VOLUME

VOL. 1:	1–89	VOL. 5:	360–449	VOL. 9:	720–809	VOL. 13:	1080–1169
VOL. 2:	90–179	VOL. 6:	450–539	VOL. 10:	810–899	VOL. 14:	1170–1259
VOL. 3:	180–269	VOL. 7:	540–629	VOL. 11:	900–989	VOL. 15:	1260–1349
VOL. 4:	270–359	VOL. 8:	630–719	VOL. 12:	990–1079	VOL. 16:	1350–1439

N

O

P

PAGE NUMBERS FOR EACH VOLUME

VOL. 1:	1-89	VOL. 5:	360–449	VOL. 9:	720–809	VOL. 13:	1080–1169
VOL. 2:	90–179	VOL. 6:	450–539	VOL. 10:	810–899	VOL. 14:	1170–1259
VOL. 3:	180–269	VOL. 7:	540–629	VOL. 11:	900–989	VOL. 15:	1260–1349
VOL. 4:	270–359	VOL. 8:	630–719	VOL. 12:	990–1079	VOL. 16:	1350–1439

Q

R

S

PAGE NUMBERS FOR EACH VOLUME

VOL. 1: 1–89	VOL. 5: 360–449	VOL. 9: 720–809	VOL. 13: 1080–1169
VOL. 2: 90–179	VOL. 6: 450–539	VOL. 10: 810–899	VOL. 14: 1170–1259
VOL. 3: 180–269	VOL. 7: 540–629	VOL. 11: 900–989	VOL. 15: 1260–1349
VOL. 4: 270–359	VOL. 8: 630–719	VOL. 12: 990–1079	VOL. 16: 1350–1439

T

U

V

W

PAGE NUMBERS FOR EACH VOLUME

VOL. 1:	1–89	VOL. 5:	360–449	VOL. 9:	720–809	VOL. 13:	1080–1169
VOL. 2:	90–179	VOL. 6:	450–539	VOL. 10:	810–899	VOL. 14:	1170–1259
VOL. 3:	180–269	VOL. 7:	540–629	VOL. 11:	900–989	VOL. 15:	1260–1349
VOL. 4:	270–359	VOL. 8:	630–719	VOL. 12:	990–1079	VOL. 16:	1350–1439

Y

Z

THE AMERICAN HERITAGE NEW ILLUSTRATED HISTORY OF THE UNITED STATES

PUBLISHED BY DELL PUBLISHING CO., INC.

George T. Delacorte, Jr., *Publisher* Helen Meyer, *President*
William F. Callahan, Jr., *Executive Vice-President*

Walter B. J. Mitchell, Jr., *Project Director;* Ross Claiborne, *Editorial Consultant;* William O'Gorman, *Editorial Assistant;* John Van Zwienen, *Art Consultant;* Rosalie Barrow, *Production Manager*

CREATED AND DESIGNED BY THE EDITORS OF AMERICAN HERITAGE MAGAZINE

James Parton, *Publisher;* Joseph J. Thorndike, Jr., *Editorial Director;* Bruce Catton, *Senior Editor;* Oliver Jensen, *Editor;* Richard M. Ketchum, *Editor, Book Division;* Irwin Glusker, *Art Director*

ROBERT R. ENDICOTT, *Project Editor-in-Chief*

James Kraft, *Assistant Editor;* Nina Page, Evelyn H. Register, Lynn Marett, *Editorial Assistants;* Lina Mainiero, *Copy Editor;* Murray Belsky, *Art Director;* Eleanor A. Dye, *Designer;* John Conley, *Assistant*